THE GHOSTS, SPIRITS AND SPECTRES OF SCOTLAND

THE GHOSTS, SPIRITS AND SPECTRES OF SCOTLAND

FRANCIS THOMPSON

BELL PUBLISHING COMPANY · NEW YORK

CONTENTS

INTRODUCTION

THE dictionary definition of 'ghost' is: 'an apparition, wraith, disembodied spirit of the dead,
manifesting itself to the senses of the living'. This
is an almost matter-of-fact description such as,
perhaps, a sceptical scientist would produce, in that
the phenomenon of the ghost had no basis in any
of the natural laws known to him. But, as the many
thousands of stories and authenticated reports of
'ghosts' prove, there are other factors to be considered, such as past tragedy, retentive and long-
lingering personalities, personal crises and so on,
which have in one way or another implanted their
unmistakable imprint on their surroundings. All
these are 'unscientific' in that they do not provide
the scientist with anything concrete, with which
he can even begin to devise suitable experimental
methods and techniques which would yield results
and from which conclusions could be drawn to add
to our knowledge of the ghost. It is the author's
own opinion that an essential factor in any ghost
'experiment' is the experimenter's or investigator's
ability to control time in other dimensions, something which Man, for all his excellent technological
advances, is still unable to take within his grasp.

Those who have seen or experienced ghosts, or
ghostly manifestations, or those who have second-
sight, indicate to us that there is a vast new world

to be explored if only we were able to do more than beat an already well-worn track up to the doorway of that world and take that fateful and decisive step over the threshold.

Another point about the dictionary definition quoted above is that it describes only one type of ghost; whereas the experience of many people proves that there are also ghosts of the living and of the dying. Those with second-sight may in fact be seeing the mature spirit forms of those not yet born. Thus, despite the fact that literature, from Plutarch, Socrates, Pliny and Cicero, and the oral and literary traditions of non-European societies whose cultures are so different from our own, includes mentions of the ghost, we are still as much in the dark in the twentieth century as were our forefathers and ancestors in prehistoric times, to whom the ghost was a despot which ruled on the basis of fear distilled in the minds of the living of the dark unknown.

A ghost, if seen, can be said to be a hallucination, in that it gives the impression of the presence of a real person, in flesh, blood and usually clothes. But no such person, in flesh, blood and clothes, is actually there. Thus, it can be said that every ghost is a hallucination. This tends to be the modern thinking about ghosts. Spirits tend also to be associated with visions of insanity, delirium, drugs, drink, remorse or anxiety. Yet, the records show that persons healthy in both mind and body also experience ghosts.

Every hallucination is a perception, as good and true a sensation as if there were a real object there.

The object happens *not* to be there, and that is all. The visitations experienced are often hard both to explain and to understand. Often the sightings are extraordinarily complete; the fact that many of the sightings are reported as being veridial (that is, as coinciding with real events such as accidents, deaths, etc., of the persons seen) is an additional complication of the phenomenon. The old doctrine and belief about ghosts was that they were actual spirits of the living or of the dead, freed from the flesh or the grave. This may be an over-simplification of the unintellectual. At the time of the Reformation, writers, especially Protestant writers, preferred to look on apparitions as the work of deceitful devils who masqueraded in the aspect of the dead or the living, or made up phantasms out of 'compressed air.'

By the eighteenth century, 'common-sense' approaches were made to the subject. All 'apparitions' were dismissed as 'dreams or hoaxes', or illusions caused by the misinterpretation of real objects. Modern science admits the possibility of hallucinations occasionally in the sane and healthy and tends to admit the existence of apparitions. Often the question is asked whether the appearances of ghosts have any provoking mental cause outside the minds of the people who experience them — any cause in the minds of others, alive or dead.

One of the most dedicated bodies established to prove or disprove the ghost is the Society for Psychical Research (SPR). It was founded in 1882, primarily as a sceptic society. It attempted to define standards, to measure and assess the imponderable, to make evidence and information conform as nearly as possible to scientific standards and controls. Its supporters included many eminent scientists of the day, among them Sir Oliver Lodge, Gilbert Murray, Henri Bergson. The Society gave itself a clear mandate:

1. An examination of the nature and extent of any influence which may be exerted by one mind upon another, apart from any generally recognised mode of perception.

2. The study of hypnotism and the forms of so-called mesmeric trance, with its alleged insensivity to pain; clairvoyance and other allied phenomena.

3. A critical revision of Reichenbach's researches with certain persons called 'sensitive', and an enquiry whether such persons possess any power of perception beyond a highly exalted sensibility of the recognised sensory organs.

4. A careful investigation of any reports resting on strong testimony regarding apparitions at the moment of death, or otherwise, or regarding disturbances in houses reputed to be haunted.

5. Any inquiry into the various physical phenomena commonly called spiritualistic; with an attempt to discover their causes and general laws.

6. The collection and collation of existing materials bearing on the history of these subjects.

An important event in the history of psychical research was the SPR Census of Hallucinations, conducted in 1880-1890. Its questionnaire was given a very wide circulation and of some 17,000 replies received, about ten per cent answered " yes " to the question: ' Have you ever, when believing yourself to be completely awake, had a vivid impression of seeing or being touched by a living or inanimate object, or of hearing a voice; which impression, so far as you can discover, was not due to say external physical cause? '.

From an analysis of the replies received, it emerged that hallucinations of living persons were twice as numerous as those of the dead; in addition, the number of instances in which the ghosts of dead people had appeared elsewhere at the moment of their deaths was no less than 440 times that which could be expected according to the law of probabilities and sound mathematical deduction. The Census confirmed that there was an extraordinary prevalence of ghosts and haunting in Britain and that apparently normal people see or experience such things.

For nearly a century the SPR has collected a mass of evidence of one kind or another which it has investigated to find that there is a positive element of the unexplained and unexplainable hidden away among the many stories and reports of ghosts and hauntings.

Fear of the dead, in particular, has ever dominated the human mind, and attempts to establish communication with the spirit world are integral in religious belief. Consequently, for so long as men fear death there will be ghosts. But these spirits of the past form only one part of the whole world of strange things which will occupy the mind of Man for many generations to come. It is argued by some that the ghost is a reflection of certain permanent attitudes in the human mind, a projection of that mind into a distorted image on a screen by the human imagination. If this is so, then the implication is surely that Man has within him (as is proved by those among us who are exceptionally gifted) those essential factors which make for effective communication with aspects, almost other dimensions, of life of which we are as yet virtually unaware.

Ghosts in Scotland are a fairly mixed bunch. They range from the true conservative to the spirit which offers real violence to the living. The former spirit confines the character of its hauntings to the limits which seem to be recognised for ' official ' haunting. This spirit tends to regard innovation with considerable mistrust, aware that any progress will sound, perhaps for a second time, a death knell from which it can never hope to recover. This may account for the fact that the ghosts experienced in our times tend to be less than one thousand years old. One hears rarely, indeed if at all, of ghosts of stone-age men, or of those who lived in prehistoric times. It would satisfy many, for instance, to hear of a sighting of a Pictish ghost, if only to obtain some details of the kind of the society which these people, now largely unknown, once established in Scotland. There are, however, exceptional sightings of very old ghosts. In 1819, at Leng in Fife, it was decided to investigate the old story of a ghost in silver armour which had often been seen in the vicinity of a tumulus. During the excavation of the site, many fragments of silver mail came to light. Even more interesting was the discovery of a skeleton enclosed in golden armour in 1832, at Bryn yr Ellyllon, the Hill of the Fairies, in Flintshire, Wales. The excavation followed local stories of a ghost in gold. The armour found is now in the British Museum.

The more violent spirit falls into the category of those ghosts which have perhaps found themselves unable to accept a rigid code of haunting law and put themselves voluntarily beyond its pale. They become terrifying spectres able to interfere with the living, to the extent of controlling them and their actions, and to possess them. In this latter case, the help of the specialist, the exorcist, is needed to utter the necessary words of command over the spirit to ' bid it depart ' from the living.

Scotland being a Celtic country, it is of interest to establish the character of the Scottish ghost, and, more particularly, the Highland ghost which often displays peculiar, almost parochial, tendencies.

The other-world of Celtic British once reflected the dreams of ancient warriors; it was a place of happiness, of continuous feasting and love-making; warfare occupied the residual energies of its occupants. This place was the Celtic heaven. The other place, to which all outcast Celtic souls were relegated, was typically inhospitable and tenanted by demons, giants and ghosts, and in which there was no peace at all.

Later, perhaps as Scotland lost her hold of her definite Celtic character, and after Gaelic had been chased from the Court and Church in the 13th century, Scottish ghosts tended to lose their racial characteristics and become no greatly different from the ghosts of other nations. The Highlands of Scotland, however (perhaps because the Gaelic language, the material and cultural link with Scotland's Celtic past, still has, even today, a strong hold on the communities there), have produced a crop of ghosts which tend to display characteristics which must have been common to the spirits in other parts of the country.

What can be called the ' Celtic ghost ' has certain affinities with the Roman and Greek ghost, which is reasonably acceptable in view of the close relationship by locality and descent that existed between the three races. There is, of course, very little evidence to support this. However, the descriptions of the funerals of the early Celts and the rites of burial point to a somewhat more realistic belief in a future life than had either the Greeks or the Romans; the actual records of belief (such as the money loans that were given on condition that they should be repaid in the next world) give strength to this view. Caesar wrote: ' Their funerals are magnificent and costly, considering their civilisation; and all that they think was dear to them when alive they put in the fire, even animals; and shortly before this generation, the slaves and dependents that they considered to have lived were burned along with them in the regular performance of funeral rites.'

Diodorus, Caesar's contemporary, says: 'For among them the opinion of Pythagoras prevails, that the souls of men are immortal, and in the course of a fixed number of years they live again, the soul entering another body. Accordingly, at the burial of the dead, some cast letters addressed to their departed relatives upon the funeral pile, under the belief that the dead will read them.'

Another writer confirms Diodorus: 'They burn and bury along with the dead whatever is of use to them when live; business accounts and the payment of debt were passed on to the next world, and there were some who, of their own free will, cast themselves on the funeral piles of their relatives, expecting to live along with them.'

Many old Irish legends point to the conclusion that the Celtic dead had ghosts of a more substantial character than either Classical or modern ghosts possess. The many tales of the Isles of Blest (Tir nan Og), where an earthly paradise existed, argue that the dead lived in bodies of a very sensuous nature and of an earthly kind. The heroic tales present but one or two actual cases of ghosts coming back to earth; but these are not disembodied spirits in any sense of the term. These ghosts are about as glorious and golden as when they lived and moved among men. Three such appearances are recorded: Cuchullin's ghost, conjured up by St Patrick, to meet King Leogaire, who promised to embrace Christianity if the Saint could raise Cuchullin.

There was the ghost of Fergus, raised by the Saints
of Erin, to recite the heroic tale, Tain Bó Cuailnge,
in the seventh century when it was discovered that
that excellent of epics had been lost to living man.
In the same century, Caoilte was raised to decide
a historical dispute between the poet Forgoll and a
semi-supernatural king named Mungan (who was,
however, said to be none other than Fionn himself
resuscitated). These apparitions are all similarly
characterised and described in great detail in the
tales. The description of Cuchullin and his horse-
drawn chariot indicates the substance of the ancient
Celtic ghost:

'A hero there in the chariot; a black, thick head
of hair; smoothness on it on him; I should imagine
it is a cow that licked it. A grey, jerking eye in his
head. A purple-blue tunic about him of borders of
all-white gold-withe. A brooch of red gold on his
breast; it extended over each of his two shoulders.
A white, hooded cloak about him, with a flashing
red border. A sword of gold-hilt in arrangement of
rest on his thighs; a broad grey spear on a shaft of
wild ash in his hand. A subsharp aggressive dart near
it. A purple shield with an even circle of silver, with
loop-animals of gold above his two shoulders. I
should think it was a shower of pearls that was flung
into his head. Blacker than the side of a black
cooking-spit each of his two brows; redder than ruby
his lips.'

So far as Highland ghosts are concerned, they
have tended to appear before those who were
possessed of a certain type of personality; the

personale of the seer is a particularly important factor in the effective materialisation of a spirit. That this is so is seen in some instances when the ghost appears in a certain manner. Some ghosts are at once understood to resemble certain persons from the striking likeness of the one to the other; it is not an uncommon thing for the seer to speak to the ghost, under the impression that the party recognised in the apparition is addressed. The ability to see a ghost tends to run in families. In one brief survey of instances of ghost sightings, more than one-third were seen by members of one family, or people who were closely related by the same blood. Others, like a friend of the writer, casually accepts the frequent appearance of a harmless and gentle female spirit being as an aspect of her own, more substantial life.

*   *   *

So far as was possible, the writer has tried to ensure that in the appropriate chapters of this book the instances of sightings, and the witnessing of supernatural manifestations, are authentic. Inevitably, an element of doubt exists in some cases; but these have been included to add an extra dimension of interest. Again, the broadest picture of ghosts and manifestations in Scotland has been offered to create what the writer understands is the first attempt to deal specifically with the subject of ghosts and hauntings in the Scottish context. The writer takes this opportunity of asking any reader with a recent experience to get in touch with him. With the other ' ghost ' or ' spirit ' of materialism so much on the rampage in our technological society of today, the more traditional ghost is being said to be less common than it was; but this may be due to the fact that plausible explanations of hauntings are being provided by physico-psychical scientists.

The writer wishes to thank Miss Wendy Wood and Mr Ronald MacDonald Douglas for their kind permission (the latter through Messrs Chambers of Edinburgh) to include in this book their experiences; thanks are also due to Dr John Lorne Campbell, Isle of Canna, for permission to use material from the books he has edited, dealing with Scotland's Western Isles, and from his *Strange Things,* co-authored with Mr Trevor Hall. Finally thanks are due to the Society for Psychical Research for permission to reprint material from their Proceedings.

1

GHOSTS OF THE DEAD

THE stories about ghosts of the dead are as numerous and as varied as one might expect. Many hauntings seem to have been made with a particular purpose: to put right some wrong; to inform the living of something left undone; to warn of impending disaster; to exact some kind of revenge. The following selection indicates the wide variety of ghost 'types' and the bases of their haunting activities.

The wife of a fisherman in Sleat, Skye, had recently been made a widow and was in no little distress as her husband had passed on without leaving any indication as to whether or not he had left any money which she could use to tide her over the early days of her misfortune. One night, while a storm raged outside the thick walls of her cottage, she saw her husband's ghost enter the room, clad in dripping oilskins. As she watched, quite unable to utter a word, the apparition crossed the floor of the room, in the direction of the fireplace. There the figure paused. Then, with a slow and deliberate movement, he made as if to remove a brick. He turned and, with a final gesture of farewell, he disappeared from her sight. After she had recovered from her initial shock, a strong sense of curiosity made her examine the fireplace carefully. Surely, she found a loose brick which she removed to find,

The shipwrecked sailor

in the exposed cavity, a considerable sum of money: her husband's savings of which she had known absolutely nothing. He had in fact returned from the unknown to reveal them to her.

The summer of 1873 saw a young man named Ranold, from South Uist, who was a widower, his dearly loved wife having died a few months previously. In an effort to forget his misfortune, he engaged himself as a hired man with the skipper of a fishing boat belonging to Fraserburgh. In time, the boat was fishing on a good bank some sixty miles to seaward from that town. About the end of the fishing season, while the boat was 'riding at its drift,' in the water of the bank, Ranold found himself taking his turn to watch on deck, while the rest of the crew turned in to take a well-earned rest and nap till daybreak. He relates:

'My duty on deck was to keep a strict lookout that our nets would not be tampered with, and that our lantern burned properly, so as to warn passing vessels of the boat's position, and thus prevent a collision with her. The night in question was pretty dark, and a fresh breeze of wind was blowing. After the crew went to their berths, all being quiet, I sat down with my back to the main-mast (for it had not been lowered that night, as was customary, as there were no signs of any considerable wind springing up before morning), lighted my pipe, and vacantly looked over the vast waste of water, as far as my eyes could penetrate through the darkness. I did not occupy this position for long (I confess it with shame) when I imperceptibly fell asleep.

'As to how long I slept I cannot say, but while sleeping I dreamed that my deceased wife came to me and in her usual sweet and pleasant manner, in an audible voice, said: " Ranold, Ranold, my

dear Ranold! Get up quickly and kindle your light.
If you do not do so immediately, you will be all
lost! " She spoke with such authority and serious-
ness that I instantly awoke, and, on looking around
me, I saw a large ship bearing swiftly down upon
our boat. I at once lighted a candle (for the light of
our lantern had somehow been extinguished) and
exhibited it. Fortunately my light was observed by
the huge ship, which at once changed her course
and bore past us. Had I been one minute later in
putting up a light, every soul in the boat would have
perished. Myself, and the rest of the boat's crew,
were thus providentially saved from a watery grave
by the interposition of my deceased wife.'

Sandwood Bay, some five miles south from Cape
Wrath, in north-west Sutherland, is well-known for
its ghostly associations. The Bay itself is a seven-mile
stretch of sand dunes. Though bleak in wintertime,
it is a beautiful spot in the summer months and a
popular mecca for tourists seeking somewhere off
the beaten track. The Bay is the haunting ground
of a ghostly seaman. He has been sighted many times,
but, when an investigation is made, there are no
traces of footprints in the sand which would betray
the presence of someone more substantial than a
ghost.

Once, two men from nearby Oldshoremore were
on the beach gathering driftwood. Suddenly, out
of nowhere, the figure of a sailor in uniform
appeared and commanded them to leave his property
alone. Terrified, the men dropped their load of
wood and fled from the spot. Some time later, a

farmer from Kinlochbervie was out in the vicinity of the Bay with some of his men on the lookout for stray sheep. Darkness was beginning to fall before all the animals were rounded up and, as

The rocky northern coast

the moon came out, the men noticed the outline of a tall man on the nearby rocks. Thinking it was one of the local men, they went towards the figure; but, as they drew near to him they realised that he was in fact a stranger and looked like a sailor. A few steps closer to him and the figure disappeared from their sight. A further search revealed nothing.

Several weeks after this incident, there was a severe storm off the west coast of Sutherland which caused an Irish vessel to go aground close by Sandwood Bay. A number of bodies were washed up on the beach and one of these was recognised by a local man (one of those who had been out looking for the sheep) as the sailor seen among the rocks. He was a heavily-built, black-bearded man. Since then, the mysterious sailor has regularly haunted the area.

Sandwood Cottage, nearby, has stood untenanted for many years as one of the most isolated and solitary habitations in Scotland. Many over-night campers have been disturbed by the figure of the seaman, with bearded face, peaked sailor's cap, and a tunic with brass buttons. One visitor to the cottage has had the experience of being wakened one night by the sensation of being suffocated by a thick, black mass that pressed down upon him. Even holiday-makers, who have camped overnight near the cottage, have not escaped the noises coming from the empty cottage of banging doors, windows being smashed and sounds of heavy footsteps in the building.

Fodderty Churchyard, in Ross-shire, on the way to Strathpeffer, is said to be the place where a ghost wanders each night among the graves, searching for that of her faithless lover. She is often seen wringing her hands and weeping. Those who see her are aware

of an eager questioning in her eyes as she makes
attempts to approach them. It is said that if any
person stays long enough for her to catch up with
them, to answer her questions, will meet with
misfortune; though if that person can tell the restless spirit where her faithless lover lies buried, he
will reap a great reward.

Another churchyard with the reputation of
being haunted is that beside the small church of
Kiltarlity, near Glenconvinth, Inverness-shire. On
one occasion, a woman was passing the church gate
after dark on her way to visit a married daughter.
Suddenly, she saw, as she thought, the daughter
with her husband and baby waiting to meet her.
Surprised, she pressed forward to meet them; they
disappeared. The figures seemed to be in some
distress when they reappeared. This time, the
woman walked slowly towards them, but for every
step she took, the figures kept their same distance
from her. Puzzled, the woman happened to look to
her left: the figures were there before her eyes; she
looked to the right, and saw them there also.
Realising that she was seeing ghostly forms, the
woman turned and fled.

Shortly after this, the ghostly figures were also
seen by a number of other people. In time the local
minister took notice of this and decided to investigate the cause of the manifestations. One night he
waited in the churchyard until long after midnight.
His patience was rewarded by a light movement in
the darkness. The figures appeared to him and,
showing signs of distress, glided past to join the

grey shadow of an old woman at a spot on the bank of the nearby river, which was notorious for flooding in springtime, with the waters often seeping into the churchyard. A thought struck the minister and he went into the church to look over the parish records. It was as he thought: some eighteen months previously a small part of the churchyard had been washed away in the flooding. The ground had contained three graves: those of a mother, her daughter who had died in childbirth, and the daughter's young husband, a wood-cutter who had been killed in an accident.

The following day, the minister organised a search along the river bank and soon a pile of bones was heaped up in the church porch. When the search had revealed all that could be found, a new funeral service was held and the bones duly given a Christian burial. A new headstone was erected, paid for by public subscription, for many desired to see the ghosts laid once and for all time. And so they were.

Perhaps the following story might indicate the beginnings of a ghost's existence. One summer's evening, a woman was in her doorway milking a cow. While she was engaged in this task, she felt her attention drawn to an object which seemed to be flying in the air. It seemed to have come from a nearby house, where there lay a person near to death's door. She was aware of the presence of the object and was able to follow it making steady progress through the warm air until it disappeared into a rock which stood some little distance from her. The object more or less resembled a man in his ordinary clothes, but the sighting was not at all distinct. The seer in this case was not a very healthy person, being prone to sickness and of a nervous disposition.

A young boy, of about seven years of age, not given to ' seeing things,' was one day playing in front of his father's house, when he ran inside, shouting that he had just seen his grandfather (who had been buried some days previously) coming along the road to the house. Alarmed, his mother questioned the boy closely and, from the description given, she was quite convinced that he had indeed seen his grandfather's spirit, there being certain details about which the lad could not have possibly known.

The following is a peculiar instance of a ghost sighting. A young man and his mother lived together. The mother eventually died, and it transpired afterwards that on her death something had been left unsettled between the pair. The man went to his minister to seek counsel and was advised to pray fervently and never to sleep without a Bible under his pillow. This advice he took and was most careful to follow it for some time until, one evening when in rather a hurry, he forgot about the minister's injunctions. That night he slept fitfully and was soon disturbed by someone trying to drag him from his bed. He recognised his dead mother's face in the form of his visitant. In some great terror the man made a promise to the spirit, when the interference ceased. The man later carried out his promise, to settle what unfinished business had remained between him and his mother, and was never afterwards disturbed.

A man who had been engaged on some smuggling operations late last century went missing for some time and his relatives became anxious about his non-appearance. They got up a search party and traced his normal route over the hills, but found no trace until, after he had been missing a day and a night, they found him drowned in a pool of water, his horse still grazing quietly nearby. Though this might seem straightforward, the most peculiar part of the mishap remains to be told. When the smuggler had left home, he had told his sister to go to a certain place with his dinner if he had not returned by a certain time. So she prepared the dinner and in due course waited for her brother's appearance. When the time had arrived and gone, she began to pack the food. As she did so, she fancied she saw her brother pass the window as if he were about to come into the house. She turned to her mother and said that there was now no need for her to pack the food as Ewan had come home. But Ewan did not come in, and their anxiety for him increased accordingly, culminating in the search which eventually found his body.

A young woman was one night sitting up with her sick uncle. While he slept quietly she passed the long hours reading a book. Then, for no particular reason, she chanced to look up towards the door and saw the figure of an old woman staring in the direction of the sick-bed. It disappeared almost at once. In some state of fear, the young woman rose to leave the room, when her uncle woke to ask her if she had just seen his mother in the room. She had, in fact, been dead for many years.

A country churchyard in the Highlands

Somewhere in the vicinity of a country churchyard in the Highlands, a young man was, one winter evening, walking past when his attention was drawn to the figure of another well-dressed young man, wearing a gold chain. This figure, however, was moving along quite fast and the onlooker was unsure whether it was on the earth or in the air. As he looked further, he saw the figure glide over the churchyard from one corner until it came to a grave near the south-west part where, to his amazement, there was another figure, dressed in white, which rose out of the ground and shook hands with the one just come, after which they separated: the dressed ghost returning as it came to disappear altogether, while the shrouded one sank into its grave.

There was a great deal of speculation about this sighting at the time and many theories were put forward to explain it. That which gained most support was that the dressed ghost was the spirit of someone, perhaps dying in some far-off land, with a last wish that he be buried beside the person whose bones already tenanted the grave. Not long after the sighting, a funeral took place in the same churchyard and the young man who had experienced the manifestations was convinced that among the mourners was a person dressed in a manner which was remarkably similar to that which the gliding ghost was seen to wear.

Spirits wander about the surface of the earth for many years with a desire to unburden themselves. Many years ago, a carrier for the district of Ness, in the north of Lewis, was making his way home from Stornoway. He had to pass the village of Galson near to a large slab of rock where a pedlar was supposed to have been murdered and buried. The carrier was on foot, leading his horse, when, as he approached the stone, he felt a presence close to him. He looked round and saw a figure dressed in the fashion of a pedlar of half a century previously. The spirit asked the man to stop. The latter, how-ever, had a clean cold fear on his heels and started to run. But the ghost laid hold of him and he was forced to sit on the slab to hear how the pedlar had been murdered. How much time he spent sat there the carrier did not know, but he was glad when the cold light of dawn broke on the horizon and caused the pedlar's ghost to fade away, still recounting the details of his death and the sadness he had borne ever since.

The following unusual ghost tale has a South Uist setting. One New Year's Day, at Daliburgh, at the south end of the island, two rival shinty teams prepared for their usual annual contest. The *camanachd* was played with the skill and fervour associated with the game, until, towards the end, a dispute arose between the two team captains on a point of ruling. One of the captains, Iain, became so angry that he raised his club and was about to strike the other a heavy blow when his eye caught sight of a tall, well-built man in dark clothing approaching him at a quick walking pace. The man beckoned him to accompany him to the beach nearby. Iain was so seized by fascination that, without any hesitation, he left the field of play, while the members of both teams were overcome with no other desire than to leave the place in a hurry. All had felt somehow that the incident was more than unusual. Strangers in a small place are so noticeable; yet this man had never been seen before.

As the stranger approached, Iain noticed that his feet did not touch the ground, but seemed to glide over the small pebbles. Despite his reputation for fearlessness and courage, Iain began to tremble. But the stranger put him at ease by saying that he was, as Iain suspected, a ghost who had interfered with the dispute on the field of play. The man, when alive, represented a member of Iain's family, though this was the first time that Iain had seen his likeness. The ghost then required Iain to act as a contact between him and the living and required that Iain meet him frequently, promising misfortune if he should refuse.

From that day onwards, Iain was under a compulsion to meet the spectre. He tried to escape the ghost by moving to another part of the island, but to no avail. The ghost discovered him the next evening and exercised the same control over him as he had always done. What transpired between Iain and the ghost was never revealed. Except that one day Iain said to the others that the ghost had indicated that he would die in a house in a place which was then nothing but a mossy waste, without house or hut from end to end. Some years later, without any reference to what the ghost had forecast — for he had forgotten the incident — Iain did indeed build a house in the place mentioned and lived there to a ripe old age. The account of Iain and the ghost (Iain belonged to a well-known family in South Uist and his strange relationship was not unknown to his neighbours) was for many years after his death, one of the tales told round the fire. Even today, the incident is as yet only half forgotten.

One night a man named John was walking home to his native village of Laxay, from nearby Keose, in Lewis, when he arrived at a bridge crossing a small burn. He was about to step on the bridge when his eye caught sight of a strange light nearby. Thinking

it was someone from his own village with a torch-
light, he called out, but got no answer. He called
out again and this time the response was a flaring
of the light and its lengthening vertically to the
height of a man. Again, thinking that someone was
playing a trick, John called out a third time. No
answer. So he went over to the light to grapple with

. . . he arrived at a bridge crossing a small burn . . .

it and was suddenly confronted by a large dark
form which began to wrestle with him. Try as he
might, John was unable to come to grips with his
opponent, though his opponent's grip was not so
uncertain. After a time, the struggle brought John
near to the edge of the burn. As he lay on the ground,

with the water gurgling in his ear, he, in a last desperate attempt for his life, managed to say : ' God have mercy on me! '

Instantly, his opponent relaxed the hold which had kept John firmly on the ground. As he recovered, John saw that he had been fighting with a ghost. Forced by the ghost's presence, John sat down on the bridge wall to hear what the ghost had to say.

The ghost had been a drover from the Scottish mainland who, some years previously, had visited Lewis to buy cattle. With this end in view, he had visited Laxay to look at some beasts. There he met up with a local man, who suspecting that the drover carried a good purseful of money to purchase cattle, he set upon him at a spot close by and murdered him. He robbed the body before burying it beside the burn, at the place where the present bridge was later erected. The drover's body was never found and the murderer had gone unpunished. The ghost, however, said that the gables of the house in which the murderer's relatives still lived could be seen from the bridge, and that the murderer's lineal descendant had since left the village to take a job on the Scottish mainland. After the encounter, John managed to make his way home and alarmed his own relatives, who were waiting up, by being violently sick as soon as he entered the house, and being confined to bed for a week with an illness which defied the local doctor's attempts to analyse.

While this story may seem to mirror some other tales about encounters with the ghosts of pedlars and similar itinerants, the family of John (a fictitious name) still lives in the neighbouring village of Keose.

The following story is of the Rev. Thomas MacKay, who was minister of Lairg, in Sutherland, and who, during his lifetime usually wore full clerical dress. He died in 1803. One summer's day in 1826, two young girls were sitting in the manse dining room when they heard a step advancing to the door. At once the door opened and they saw standing in the doorway a thin, old man, dressed in black, with knee breeches and buckles, black silk stockings and shoes with buckles. With a stare that took in everything in the room, he stood for a few moments and then walked out. After they had recovered from their astonishment, the girls mentioned the incident to the resident minister who, curious to know who his visitor was, searched the house, but found no one.

Some older people, having heard the girls' description of the old minister, knew it at once to be that of the deceased Rev MacKay. About ten years after this incident, the same two girls, having reached womanhood, met one of the Rev MacKay's grand-daughters; on seeing one of the grand-daughters, one of the women exlaimed: 'How like you are to your grandfather!' To which the other replied: 'So the old people tell me, but how did you know that, for he died before you were born?' The woman had in fact recognised the grand-daughter's resemblance to the old minister who had appeared to her in the manse.

The following is an authentic, though curious story. A young man, who assisted at a shooting lodge, was having his hair cut by the coachman, when the latter remarked: 'I see that on the side of your head there has grown a lump which was not there when I last cut your hair.'

On hearing this, the young man grew pale and almost fainted. When the coachman enquired what ailed him, he replied: 'Now I can tell my story, but ask some others to come in and hear it also.' This was done and the young man began:

'You know that it is part of my duty to cross Cnoc-na-moine very often after it is dark, and many a time I did it, but, although there were strange stories about the little hollow near the top, I did not think much about them, and if they did come into my mind, I just whistled to myself to keep up my courage. Exactly a year ago today I was going home along the path as usual, but I felt quite cheery, as I had got a good tip from the gentleman who was leaving the lodge. Suddenly, just at the nasty place, I was met by a big, strong fellow, well dressed in full Highland garb, but just a little old fashioned I thought. He said nothing, but just kept looking at me. I said in Gaelic: "In the name of the Trinity, if you come from heaven or hell, and have anything to say, I shall listen."

'The ghost replied: "That is why I am here. I was murdered on this very spot one hundred and twenty-four years ago, and I am allowed to visit it once a year ever since on the anniversary of the murder to tell it to someone ere I can be allowed to rest in the place I have been sent to. I could never meet anyone before who spoke to me, and I want to tell you that I was coming home from the south with some money when two brothers of the name of A . . . ,who lived at B . . . , set on me, killed me, took my money and then buried my body. As my people did not know that I was coming the murderers were never found out, and were never suspected to be what they were. They built a good house with the money, and their descendants occupy it to this day, and now I want you to tell the people of the place who murdered me."

' He stopped, and I said: " Mr A . . . will hate me and try to do me harm if I tell such a story of his ancestor, and they are good enough neighbours to me just now."

' The soldier replied: " If you don't tell you will find that I can do you harm. You will find that if you keep my secret soon a lump will begin to grow on your head and will press on your brain so that you will become mad, and in your madness you will tell the secret. It is better for you to tell it before that happens."

' The old soldier then suddenly seemed to sink into the earth. I went home but told no one till now, and now I pray that the lump on my head may disappear since I have cleared my conscience; and the soldier said he would never be seen again once it became known who had murdered him.'

After the story spread through the parish, it was expected that the families involved would dispute its authenticity, but they did not. If the ghost soldier seeked revenge he did not get it. But since then the path at Cnoc-na-Moine has ever been given a wide berth at nights.

In 1869, a man from the parish of Farr, in Sutherland, had occasion to post a letter. It was a distance of over two miles to the post office, most of the way being across some hills. As he approached the main road, he was taken hold of by some unaccountable fear and a feeling of imminent danger. So alarmed did he become that he thought of turning back, though the day was bright and calm. Suddenly he was confronted by a man well known to him, whose face and hands were a mass of congealed blood. He asked the injured man what had happened to him, but was waved off. He, however, noticed that one of the man's fingers was broken.

The injured man told him that he had left his mother's house two days before, intending to visit some friends in a neighbouring village, and took a path which ran along the cliffs so as to shorten his journey. At the lower end of his mother's croft, which ran down to the cliffs, his foot slipped and he fell to the bottom of the rocks. He stated further that he had lain there for two days and two nights and that once he had heard, carried by the wind, his mother's voice as she spoke to a neighbour, who was helping her to cut some corn above the cliff. With a deep sigh, the ghost said : ' It was cruel of you to leave me there so long.' Then he vanished from sight.

The man, startled and still half-frozen with fear, hurried on his way and arrived at the post office where it was seen that he was suffering from some kind of mental anguish. He was induced to tell the cause of his distress, and after some inquiries, the postmaster, in the company of the minister and others, hurried to the spot indicated. There they found the lifeless body of the man whose mysterious appearance had so terrified the other man. One side of the head was badly injured, and the middle finger of the left hand was broken. Everything was as described an hour before the body was discovered.

A well-to-do Shetland fishcurer once died rather suddenly. One morning, several days after the burial, his son entered the shop to be confronted by the figure of his father standing by the desk, apparently deep in the study of some accounts. He disappeared immediately. But later the same figure was seen by workmen in the deceased man's curing sheds.

The following indicates a common request by ghosts to be re-interred in places which are more comfortable. A boat on the west coast of Scotland was wrecked and three of her crew were drowned. The bodies were found and, according to custom, they were not carried to the churchyard but buried on the spot, near the scene of the wreck. Soon afterwards, three spirits were often seen to hover near the burial place. The local folk, determined to rid themselves of the apparitions, decided to disinter the bodies and found the graves full of water. After re-burial in dry earth, the apparitions were satisfied and never bothered the living in the district.

A similar story is told of a woman, from the same

district, whose spirit appeared to several folk, including her husband, a few days after her burial asking that her body be removed on account of the water that was collecting in her grave. The grave was opened and was indeed found to be full of water. A drain was constructed beneath the grave. The body was reburied and her ghost was never seen again.

The following story is yet another authentic instance of a sighting of a manifestation, and is probably more unusual for its sequel. A friend of the writer was employed in Stornoway, Lewis, to which town he made his way to work daily from the village of Grimshader, a few miles to the south of Stornoway. The road from the village crosses the southern part of Arnish Moor to meet the main Harris-Stornoway Road. For many years there had been a local tradition that the area near to the road junction was haunted, having been the scene of a murder. But there had never been anything substantial to confirm this tradition.

One evening, when B was returning from Stornoway, in a small van, he had no sooner turned off the main road onto the smaller Grimshader Road when he became aware of a spirit figure beside him; the face was indistinct, but there was no doubt about its supernatural character. The figure's presence remained for a mile or so, then disappeared. While one such experience was unnerving enough, the matter became quite depressing to B when he found that each night as he turned off the main road, the same ghostly manifestation accompanied him along for about a mile. Even when on a motor-bike, the figure would materialise and travel silently alongside. In the end, B resorted to a small boat with an outboard motor, to make the journey by sea to Stornoway, a distance of about five miles.

A few years ago, since when B had left Lewis for another part of the British Isles, a man's body was discovered near the junction of the Grimshader road with the main road to Stornoway. The find consisted of human remains, clothing and personal objects. Due to the action of the peat acid, the bones were reduced to the consistency of rubbery seaweed. The woollen cloth required several washings and then treated with a lanolin solution in order to replace lost fats in the material. The skeleton was that of a man of between 20 and 25 years of age. The opinion of the Department of Forensic Medicine, in Edinburgh University, was that ' . . . the appearances seen in the posterior part of the right parietal bone are consistent with, and indeed suggestive of a localised depressed fracture such as, would result from the impact of an object having a defined striking surface. The position of this fracture would be consistent with a blow wielded by a right-handed assailant attacking from the rear.' Surely this could mean that the young man had been murdered. The clothing is dated c. 1700.

The local tradition is that two youths attending a school at Stornoway went to the moors on a bird-nesting expedition. They quarrelled when sharing out the spoil, and one of them felled the other by a blow on the head with a stone. When he realised that his companion was dead, he buried him and fled to Tarbert, Harris, whence he made his way to the south and took up a seafaring life. Many years afterwards his ship put into Stornoway and he went ashore, probably intending to remain incognito. But he was recognised, convicted of murder and hanged on Gallows Hill.

As often told, the story was provided with a dramatic denouement. On coming ashore from his ship, the guilty man entered one of the inns on the waterfront of the town and ordered a meal. While waiting for it to be served, he noticed that the handles of the cutlery on the table were of an unusual design. He was told that the handles were made from some sheep bones found in a hole on the Arnish Moor. He handles the cutlery and is terror-stricken when the bone handles ooze blood. This refers to the motif of the corpse beginning to bleed when touched by the murderer. For many years the scene of the murder was believed to be haunted and people avoided that particular stretch of the road after dark.

The ghost was often to be seen, particularly about four miles north of Soval, in the vicinity of a grey rock, white in part towards the top, near a little stream, on the right-hand side of the road coming back from Stornoway.

The body in the peat of Arnish Moor was found so near the scene of the almost legendary crime that it is not unreasonable to link the two. And that the man was murdered, there is little doubt. What remains, perhaps, to be explained is the reason for the spirit manifestation which confronted my friend. But, as seems to be the wish of most manifestations, the ghost merely desired to speak of the crime which deprived him of his life.

2

GHOSTS OF THE LIVING

WHILST many people would willingly accept that ghosts are spirits of the dead, they would probably be less inclined to accept the fact that there are also spirits of the living which are no less frequently seen. From the scientific viewpoint, it may be said that only the living can have ghosts, in that living bodies possess the energy sources to produce extra-physical manifestations. Phantoms of the living — our Scottish 'wraiths' — have received from the Society for Psychical Research a scientific, or quasi-scientific, explanation by the invention of the word 'telepathy.' Its etymological force is 'feeling at a distance,' and is intended to denote the mysterious influences and impressions which one mind is able to exert upon another mind, apparently without the usual means of communication, and even at a far distance. The modern term of 'extra-sensory perception' is an aspect of this subject which is undergoing serious investigation at seats of higher learning, such as in Edinburgh University.

Experiment has tended to prove that telepathy — the supersensory transference of thoughts and feelings from one mind to another — is a fact in nature (supersensory is defined as being independent of the recognised channels of sense). Many verified testimonies prove that phantasms (impressions, voices or figures) of persons undergoing some crisis — especially death or impending disaster — are perceived by their friends and relatives with a frequency which mere chance cannot properly explain.

The distinction between spirits of the dead and those of the living have been known and accepted for many centuries. In the Highlands of Scotland for instance, the word 'ghost' is applied only to a spirit of the departed, while the spirit of a living person is terms 'wraith' (Gaelic: *samha*—likeness; or *tamhasg*—apparition). There has not been, however, any clean-cut division in the use of these words. It is an interesting fact that in the Highlands there are more stories about the ghost based on the wraith idea than on the ghost as a spirit of the dead. Most of the appearances of wraiths indicate the impending death of the person whose spirit has been seen, or that the person was in some kind of crisis which so stressed the mental and subconscious to the extent that the personality had parted company with the body to appear before some relative or close friend. There are people today who tell of their strange ability to leave themselves in a spirit form. The author has a very close relative who, undergoing a period of acute pain and mental anguish, rose above herself and watched, mirror-like, her physical being on the bed. She describes this state as being one of almost ecstatic freedom from the stresses she had been experiencing.

Wraiths and portents of impending disaster present themselves to only one sense at a time: a person is seen, the person's voice only is heard in some kind of unearthly cry, or a man gets entangled in a phantom funeral and is forced to turn aside by the crush of the people in the procession.

In the Highlands, the term ' spirits of the living ' is often used to describe the appearances of people who are alive and well — but who are in fact elsewhere. The common Highland belief is that these spirits show themselves to second-sighted persons, very frequently before the arrival of a stranger or a visitor, expected or unexpected. These appearances of those living but absent, whether caused by some mental action of the person who appears or not, are, at least, unconscious on his part. Catholic theology recognises, under the name of ' bilocation,' the appearance of a person in one place when he is really in another. A few cases exist in which a living person is said, by a voluntary exertion of mind, to have made himself visible to a friend at a distance.

Last century, a sailor in the East Indies became used to seeing the wraith of a young woman in the forecastle-head of his ship. When at last he plucked up courage to approach her she called out to him: *" Cum do ghreim, Aindrea, 's chan eagal duit "* (Keep your hold, Andrew, and there is no fear of you). In time the sailor arrived at his home town of Wick and no sooner had he disembarked when he saw the very woman whose wraith he had met on the ship. He eventually met up with her and later married her. This couple lived for many years in Farr.

Another story tells of a man who emigrated to America. There he was constantly bothered to the point of irritation by the wraith of a very close acquaintance, who was still living in the old country. After some years, this same friend emigrated and on his arrival in the States thought first to visit his old friend. The latter was cutting wood at the time of his arrival. He looked up and saw the real man approaching him. In a fit of anger he picked up his axe and rushed on the oncoming figure, which he would have cut down had he not been held by some people nearby. When he shook hands with his old friend he realised that he would be bothered no more by the wraith. In this particular instance, almost as if an exception to an accepted rule, no disaster befell the friend.

Wraiths differ from the ghosts of the dead in that they appear during the day or night, as distinct from the latter which invariably keep to the hours of darkness. One young man from Loch Tayside was sent out by his mother to look after some cattle grazing on an upland some distance away from the village. A sale was going on in a nearby farmyard which so excited his curiosity that he left the care of his cattle and went to see what was going on. But no sooner had he joined up with the crowd when he saw his mother standing by the gate to the yard. He hid himself as well as he could and made off to get back to his cattle-herding again. That evening, when he got home, he learned that not only had he not been seen, but that his mother had never been near the farm sale.

Another true story tells of the housewife who paused in her work to address a vacant armchair as though a man of her acquaintance were sitting in it. This she did to the complete amazement of her family and others who were in the house at the time. The amazement was even greater when an hour after the incident the man in question visited the house and sat down in the same armchair.

A woman in Glenmoriston, Inverness-shire, was one day walking through the village when she noticed a neighbour coming towards her. Just as she was preparing to greet her, the neighbour disappeared. On another occasion she saw one of the district's gentry walking in front of her dressed in his Sunday clothes; she noted particularly a red vest which he was wearing. As she wondered why the man was so dressed on a week-day, he vanished from her sight. In both these cases the parties whose wraiths had been seen died shortly afterwards.

Yet another Glenmoriston story, duly authenticated, tells how two men were passing across a small stream near the village when one of them whispered to his companion that he had just seen the ghost of R . . . , who at that time was very low in health. The other man looked in the direction indicated but saw nothing. When the men later returned to the village they were met with the news that R . . . had just died; further investigation proved that the death had occurred at the time when the wraith was seen.

Again in the Glenmoriston district, a farm grieve one night left his father's house to go to the farm where he was employed. About half-way he felt uneasy but was unable to explain why. In a short time, however, he discerned the figure of a woman not far from him and which moved along with him. This woman was very ill at the time and she died soon after her wraith was seen.

There is the true story of a man who saw his own wraith. One night, at Halloween, a young man went out to the yard beside his home to perform some of the traditional and superstitious rites whereby a future bride was supposed to appear. But instead of a woman's form, he was met by his own phantom appearance. This unusual event was followed by the death of the young man shortly afterwards. In Strathspey a young woman, at the time enjoying very good health, dreamed that a coffin, which she described in every detail, was brought into the house and placed in a certain way on some chairs. Two days later the girl died suddenly and her dream, in every respect, came true. This time, however, no wraith was seen, only the circumstances of the coffin.

One day, in Ballachulish, an old man was sitting on a felled tree beside a steep track in a quarry. He was accompanied by a young boy, and the two were in deep conversation when, suddenly, the old man jerked the boy to one side and pushed him over to the other side of the tree trunk. The boy stared in confusion at the old man, while the latter rose and looked fixedly while muttering to himself: ' The spirits of the living are strong today! ' He then told the boy that he had seen a mass of rock fall down from a nearby height to kill some of the quarry workmen. The accident, as foretold, occurred the following day at the spot where the pair had been sitting.

Phantom funerals are the most common form of phantasmal apparitions of living people. The stories about ghost funerals are quite endless. Neil M. Gunn, the late, much-respected Highland author, used the sighting of a ghostly funeral party in his novel appropriately entitled *Second Sight* (published in 1940). Quite often the stories tell of two people walking along a road, when one suddenly becomes seized with a construction in his breathing and struggles as though to get through a large crowd of unmoving people. His companion invariably feels nothing, except to observe the other's actions. In other stories, the affected man pulls his companion to one side on account of the crowd he sees approaching them. So many times have ghostly funerals been seen that there was once an unwritten rule of the road in the Highlands: never walk in the middle of the road for fear you may find yourself in the midst of a phantom funeral party.

A man in Sutherland was walking home one night when, as he neared his house, he began to wonder why the house was just as far away with every step he took. To his surprise and dismay he found himself in a churchyard quite some distance from his home. He could hear distinctly the noise of a spade working among earth, stones and gravel. He knew then that he must have been caught up by a phantom funeral and carried to the churchyard. Later, when he got home, he heard that a neighbour woman had seen a ghostly funeral on the same road which the man had taken to walk home, thus obtaining a first-hand confirmation of his own experience.

Two men were walking along a road outside Strathpeffer, in Ross-shire, when one of them suddenly touched his friend's arm and asked him to stand aside " to allow the funeral to pass." His friend, alarmed because he could see nothing, stood aside as he was asked. He said that he was unable to see anything and was told by his companion that the latter realised that the funeral was a spectral one. " Tomorrow you will find that a funeral will pass along here to Fodderty Churchyard." The next day such a funeral did pass along the same road, and at the same hour.

One old woman, who lived in Dingwall, had the reputation of being able to see the spirits of persons known to her and is on record as stating that once she had ' seen ' a particular person who was then known to be in America. Some weeks afterwards there came news of that person's death, which had taken place (in America) on the day on which he was ' seen ' in Dingwall.

Another authenticated instance of seeing a phantom funeral is told in the Newtonmore district of Inverness-shire. This man was known for his gift, though he was always reluctant to display it or talk about what he had seen. On one occasion he was walking along a road and was about to cross a bridge when a phantom funeral met him. At the moment he involuntary stepped aside to allow the procession to pass, he received a severe kick on the leg from a horse that happened to be ridden by one of the spectre funeral party in the rear of the procession. That he got some kind of blow from the animal was unmistakeable for he felt the pain and actually limped his way home. On entering his house he told his family what had happened; but on examining his leg no bruise could be found. For the rest of the day, and during the night, he man complained continually of the severe pain in his leg. But the next day he was up as usual and, having occasion to pass along the same road and over the same bridge, he met a real funeral. As he allowed this party to pass by he noticed that a horse and rider were approaching him. Almost at the same time as he made to step back, the horse shied and kicked him severely in the leg, in the exact spot where the phantom horse had dealt him the blow the previous day. Once more he limped home and an examination found a serious bruise which this time kept him in his bed for some time.

The following incident is told by a minister of the Church of Scotland:

" A young lad, a herd-boy in the village in the Western Isles, to which I belong, was one day with me on the moors above the cultivated land, when he said he saw two men carrying a coffin between them from the wright's workshop then in sight to the doors of a house, which he mentioned. He called my attention to the vision, but I could see nothing of the kind. He described the dress the two men had on, particularly grey trousers, such as seafaring people of the place then wore. In about ten days after, an event exactly corresponding occurred."

The Western Isles

A native of the Isle of Harris relates his experience thus: " On one occasion I was out fishing till twelve or one o'clock in the morning, with several others, of whom one, a man about thirty-five, was reputed to have the Second Sight. As we were coming home, I kept to the middle of the road, thinking it was the safest place, and that no evil

could come near me there. Suddenly, the man who
had the Second Sight caught me by the shoulder and
pulled me to the side of the road. As he laid his
hand on my shoulder I saw a funeral procession —
a coffin and men carrying it. I was afterwards at that
funeral myself, and at the place where I met the
' sight ' the men were in the same order in which
I had seen them."

One woman near Loch Scavaig in Skye saw a
funeral procession, with the coffins, passing along
a hillside, where there was no road, and where no
one was ever observed to pass. After the death of
the woman, and some two years after she had
reported the ' sighting,' a boat was lost in the Loch,
and the bodies of the three persons in her were
buried near a shepherd's house beside the Loch.
The bodies were afterwards raised and carried along
in the direction the woman had pointed out as that
taken by her vision.

. At Gollanfield, some few miles from Inverness, a
family were sitting at family worship when there
came a knock to the door. The sound was heard
only by the mother and daughter. When the door
was opened, there was nothing to be seen, and
nothing further was heard. A fortnight later a
horseman knocked at the door with the end of his
whip — producing exactly the same sound as was
heard previously. Only the mother and daughter
were in the house when he called with the news that
an intimate friend had just died.

A teacher's daughter was one evening sitting in
a schoolhouse in the island of Lewis when she heard

what she thought was a cry of distress coming from the rocks in the immediate neighbourhood. When her father came into the house she told him of what she had heard and he set off immediately to search the rocks. But he found nothing. He was about to leave the shore when he himself heard a cry coming from the sea. It was so unearthly that he went into a neighbour's house for both light and human comfort. He told them of the strange incident and was curious to observe that the family were distinctly worried about the affair, though they said nothing. About a month later, the schoolmaster's neighbour's son was drowned at the spot where the cry seemed to have come. After the tragedy, the family said that they had been worried because it was to their house the teacher had first come with the story, and they had prepared themselves for bad news. Which indeed arrived in due course.

Animals see wraiths just as often as do human beings. In one house two families lived under the same roof but in separate apartments, with a door and a passageway between them. The family in one end were startled one evening by their collie dog which, previously lying peacefully in front of the fire, jumped up and rushed to the door to make frantic efforts in an attack against some unseen object or assailant. At the same time (this was confirmed later) the family in the other end of the house were alarmed at the distinct noises they heard coming from the passageway, as if two persons were in a desperate struggle for their lives. As both families moved to investigate the matter, each not knowing the other had been disturbed, the noises ceased and the dog became quiet again.

Afterwards, both families heard that, some distance away, a madman had killed a young woman. The dog had at one time belonged to the killer, while the unfortunate victim was related to both families in the house. She had, in fact, passed through the door and passageway only a few days before her untimely death.

3

GHOSTS IN FOLKTALE
AND LEGEND

THAT the ghost has been an ever-present factor in
the patterns of life and death in many rural areas
and communities is seen in the large number of
folktales and legends which feature a spirit of some
kind or another and which have been in oral
circulation for many centuries; only in the last
century or so have they been recorded and written
down. Some ghost tales of the Highlands and
Islands are extremely old and have a thread of
continuity which goes back at least one thousand
years. In similar fashion, many localities have pre-
served stories and tales of ghosts. The Borders of
Scotland have been a rich area of ballads, many of
which feature the supernatural, perhaps in more
dramatic form than the simpler folktale.

There is a small island called Hellisay, in the
Sound of Barra, Outer Hebrides. The sea round its
shores is full of fish, a fact which has never escaped
the attention of the folk on nearby Eriskay island.
One day an Eriskay man, his son and grandson set
out for a day's fishing. After they had set their lines,

they decided to make for Hellisay to explore the place. Once on the island the grandfather made off on his own, in the direction of an empty house which had belonged to a shepherd recently evicted from Hellisay. The other two stayed on the shore beside their boat.

Looking in at one of the windows, the old man's eyes caught sight of a fine long plank of wood. As wood is a scarce commodity in the Hebrides where there are virtually no trees and the folk have to rely on what the sea throws up on the shores, he decided that it would be a good prize to take back with him to Eriskay. He managed to open the door, went into the house, gathered up the plank and made for the shore. But on the way back he was confronted by a ghost which tried to take the plank from him. The shape of the ghost was indeterminate but there was no doubt that if he wanted to keep the plank he would have to fight for it. A serious struggle followed.

In the meantime the father and son were sitting in the boat by the shore waiting for the old man to return. When he did not make an appearance, the son was told to go and look out for him. The boy did so and clambered over the high sand dunes. As he came close to the deserted house he saw his grandfather fighting with the ghost over the plank. With a spurt of sand-dust on his heels, the boy ran back to the boat, followed by his grandfather's words:

"Calum! Be as quick as you can! Tell your father to come here with the helm of the rudder. I'm here fighting with the Devil!"

"Grandfather is fighting with the Devil!" shouted the lad to his father.

"It's high time the Devil did come and take your grandfather — he should have taken him a long time ago!" was the reply from the father as he took the helm and made for the spot where the fight was going on with no ground being given or taken. As soon as the father came in sight, the ghost disappeared.

The old man sat down, apparently quite exhausted.

" Why did you not come sooner? " he asked. " I wanted to knock him one with the helm so that he'd never come back again."

But the plank, the prize, had been won, and the proud grandfather walked down to the shore with it. They were about to push off when another boat from Eriskay landed and some men from it came over to them. As they greeted them, they caught sight of the old man's plank of wood. Then they told the story of how they had searched Eriskay for a good plank of wood to make a coffin for a woman who had died the previous night. But they had not been able to find anything suitable. Now, eyeing the old man's plank, they asked if they could have it. He agreed and the plank changed hands. The Eriskay woman was put into the coffin and later buried. The Hellisay ghost was never seen again.

In some Highland ghost tales, the ghost is presented as a ghost of ' substance,' in that the figure appears as being no different from living men. Indeed, the more substantial the ghost, the older the tale seems to be; ghosts of more recent belief and origin tend to be ordinary, insubstantial and rather airy beings.

In a tale collected by J. F. Campbell, we are told of the many adventures of the ' Barra Widow's Son.' During his travels he arrived at one stage in Turkey and soon after met up with a strange sight, that of two men beating a corpse as hard as they could.

" What are you doing? " asked John, the widow's
son.

" This man was a Christian. We had eight marks
against him and since he did not pay us when he
was alive we are taking it out of his corpse."

" Well, then. If you care to leave him with me
I will pay you the eight marks."

The men, well satisfied, left John with the body.
He, as the tale goes, ' put mould and earth on him ';
that is, he committed the body to a decent grave and
burial.

Many more adventures were to befall John after
this incident before he found himself on his way
home, sailing with his lady-love, the King of Spain's
daughter. But the same ship carried a General who,
jealous of John, managed by trickery to get John
cast away on a desert island. In distress and despair,
John thought his position quite hopeless, ' hair and
beard grown over him; his shoes were worn to pulp,
without a thread of clothes on that was not gone to
rags; without a bit of flesh on him, his bones but
sticking together.'

Eventually, just when he thought his end had
come, he heard one night the sound of a boat rowing
towards the island.

" Are you there, Iain Albannaich? " asked a
voice.

Not a little afraid, for he was quite uncertain of
what to expect, John went down to the shoreline
and there found a man in a boat in the water's
edge.

" What will you give me if I take you off this

desolate island? " John was asked. " Would you give me half your kingdom, half your wife and children? "

John answered that he had no kingdom, no wife and no children. But if he had he would most certainly give them to the stranger. Anything to get off the island.

" As good as done," said the stranger. So John and the unknown man rowed away to eventually land in Spain. There John in due course recovered his lady-love and was married. By this time the stranger had vanished as mysteriously as he had appeared and was all but forgotten when, after John had become the King of Spain and the father of three sons, he re-appeared once more to confront John.

" Are you for keeping your promise? " he asked.

" Yes," said John, who then prepared to make his sacrifice to keep his old bargain.

But the stranger said: " For your willingness you can have back what you were prepared to give me. I am the man for whose body you paid the eight marks."

So saying, he vanished from John's sight for all time.

There was once a widow who had an only son. She did not wish him to marry until it was her pleasure that he should do so, and he was persuaded to promise that he would seek her permission if ever he wished to marry. One day, when it was snowing hard, she killed a bird and asked her son to leave home and look for a girl whose cheeks were as red as the blood on the snow, who had skin as white as the snow and whose foot would fit a crystal shoe she had.

So the young man started out on his quest. On the first night away from home he passed a church-yard from which some strange noises were coming. Looking over the wall he saw some men breaking up bones. These were part of a man's skeleton. Asking why they were doing this, he was told that they had a debt against the dead man and were now taking their revenge. Offering the amount of the debt, the men revealed that they in fact were as dead as the skeleton whose bones they were breaking. But, they said, their brothers and sisters still lived and he could deliver the money to them.

This the young man did. Afterwards, on his way through a dark and lonely wood, he met a man who told him that it was for him the debt had been paid. Asking the son if there was anything he needed, the ghost-man was told of the quest for a girl who would satisfy his mother's description.

"You will be successful enough," was the reply, and the son then received direction to a house where he would obtain a cloak of darkness which, when worn, would render the wearer invisible. This was the start of many adventures, all successful and rewarding, thanks to the pity of the living for the bones of the dead.

On the west coast of Lewis, a fisherman's young wife was left alone one night while her husband went out fishing. During the night she heard strange cries which so upset her that she became afraid.

When she told her husband about them on his return he laughed at her and said that the cries were most likely those of seagulls. But she said she was convinced that the cries were such that no bird could have made them.

On the following night, when her husband had gone out fishing again, the young woman heard the cries and decided to find out their origin. Clutching her rosary of shells, she followed in the direction of the cries and came upon the ghost of a drowned foreign woman, whose body had been found on the-shore and buried nearby.

The ghost told the woman that until her grave had been ' paid ' for, she could never rest, and she would be condemned to wander for ever on the shore. The woman said that though hers was a very poor fisherman's family she would see what she could do to help.

" Cut a sheaf of ripe corn from your husband's field and lay it in my grave. Then I shall be able to rest."

The woman went off to get the corn, but wondered how she could open the grave. But on her return, however, she found the ghost standing by the grave, opened to receive the ' payment.' Placing the corn in the grave, the ghost thanked the woman and, taking a clear black stone from the folds of her dress, handed it to the woman.

" Keep this and give it to your son on the day he becomes seven years old."

Saying that, she lay down in the grave, which

closed over her, to leave the woman alone save for the sounds of the nearby waves on the shore.

Some months after this a son was born to the fisherman's wife and the ghost incident was forgotten. Years passed and it was not until the son's seventh birthday that the stone was remembered and given to the boy, who was later known as *Coinneach Odhar,* the famous Highland seer of Brahan.

Loch Awe

A minister in Skye had more concern during his lifetime for his cattle than for his parish flock of people. Even after he died his ghost was often to be seen hovering around the cattle-fold. There was much discussion about this nuisance, and it fell to one old man to volunteer and lay the troublesome spirit. One night he went to the fold and waited until he caught sight of the minister's ghost. Shouting a greeting and extending his hand, the ghost came towards him. But just as it was about to shake the old man's hand, the latter substituted an iron ploughshare. Touching the cold metal, the ghost disappeared and was never seen again.

There was once a ghost who caused no end of bother to people travelling on a particular road in Lochaweside, Argyll. In the end, in desperation, the word went out for someone strong enough and with the knowledge necessary to lay the spirit. One such man was found who went to the ghost's favourite haunting spot. There he met the ghost and exorcised it in the name of Peter and Paul and all the most powerful saints. But the ghost never moved. At last the call went out:

" In the name of the Duke of Argyll, I tell you to get out of there immediately! "

And the ghost promptly disappeared and was never seen again.

4

GHOSTLY NOISES AND LIGHTS

IT may well be that those who have never had the experience of seeing some visible ghostly manifestation are compensated either by seeing strange lights or by hearing noises the origins of which are quite unaccountable. Certainly, many have claimed to have seen lights and heard noises for which they could give no satisfactory explanation. But lights and sounds are often integral parts in the bag of tricks which the mind sometimes plays on us. The sun glancing on some bright object; the strange magnifying effects which people have seen from a boat looking to the landward sky to observe moving shapes almost mirroring some movement on the land hidden from seaward; the echoes of noises on a clear, still night originating a long distance away. All these have undoubtedly raised questions when their origins were claimed to be supernatural.

The growth of interest in Unidentified Flying Objects over the years has resulted in a large body of devotees willing to accept that the significant percentage of unexplained light-based objects seen in the sky is due to non-earthly, though not necessarily supernatural, manifestations. Whether they would accept a spirit explanation for the UFO is doubtful, being determined to subject their ' sightings ' to all kinds of tests with a scientific and rational base.

There is a fairly large body of accounts of ghostly lights and sounds which defy rational explanation, and which include such subjects as death divination and second sight. Usually the appearance of lights indicates the death or forthcoming death of someone either known to the seer or else someone in the community. One man, who was not given to story-telling for its own sake, took serious views about omens seen either by himself or by others. On several nights the sounds of a strange four-oared boat were heard coming from the opposite shore of Loch Erisort, Lewis, close by his home. This, he said, presaged a death, and the inevitable occurred within two months by the arrival of two boats, each bringing a coffin to the village. On a hillside near Loch Erisort a light was often seen which was taken as a sign of the proprietor's death. The event took place within the year. On many other occasions the lights of phantom boats were seen, all omens of forthcoming deaths which came about in due time.

One man in the village of Carnish, North Uist, related how he had heard strange rappings on the walls of his store for a period of several nights. He found the sound omen confirmed when some coffin furnishings were required from his shop soon afterwards.

But the fact can often play tricks on one's imagination. Damp, mossy peat banks sometimes exude a phosphorescent glow which can be mistaken for many things. This phenomenon is due to a small plant which is found in decaying vegetation and which is common in some parts of the moors in Scotland. If it is observed as being all over a person who is walking on the moor at night, it is taken for a sign of death by drowning at sea.

The late Alasdair Alpin MacGregor tells the story of a doctor from Edinburgh who was holidaying at an inn at Broadford in Skye. After supper he decided to take a turn outside before settling down for the night. Walking along the shore in the half-light of the evening, he noticed a glow out in the bay. At first he took it to be a flare lit by some fisherman in a boat. But then he noticed that the light was travelling too smoothly for that explanation. In addition, it was travelling at a pace which indicated that it was no ordinary kind of light. Gradually the light came nearer until it touched the shoreline — then went out. The next thing of which the doctor was aware was the form of a cloaked woman, with a child in her arms, hurrying across the sand in front of him. The glimpse he caught was only a fleeting one, because the woman vanished in a moment.

Returning to his lodgings, the doctor told his host of what he had seen and asked him for some possible explanation. With some reluctance he was told of a shipwreck, which had occurred several years before, in which a woman and child had been cast ashore, both dead, at the very spot at which the doctor had seen the strange light. This occurrence is said to be seen occasionally, even in these modern times, usually on or near the anniversary of the tragedy.

Another strange light is associated with Loch Rannoch. This takes the form of a glow in the shape of a ball which has been seen skimming across the surface of the water. It always rises from the same point, travels the same short distance, and disappears in the same place. Local tradition tells of those who have observed this same light not only on the water but rolling up from the loch to climb the nearby hill known as Meall-dubh.

Balls of light or fire are also known on Loch Tay. These are more specific in spirit origin and are related in connection with a man whose two brothers died of fever while he was serving in the Army. The brothers were buried in the churchyard at Kenmore. On the return of the surviving brother from active service, he decided to re-inter the remains at Killin, at the other end of Loch Tay. The night before the proposed exhumation, two very bright balls of fire were seen rolling along the surface of the water, in the very direction to be followed the next day by the boat containing the two coffins.

Highland tradition is full of tales of ghostly noises, of which the noise of phantom coffin-making is the most common. There was once a time when scarcely a carpenter's shop existed which did not have its full quota of sights and sounds seen and heard immediately before a coffin was made. These sounds invariably occurred at night and were heard either by the carpenter himself or by a member of

his family. Wood intended for coffins is particularly
noted to be troublesome about a house or shop.
Wood is dashed to the ground; furnishings for
coffins are apt to get noisy and restless; trestles are
shifted about; and the noises of sawing, cutting and
planes shaving wood are often heard.

Corpse candles are common sights. These 'candles'
or lights are often seen flickering as they go along
their way to the churchyard. If the lights are seen
close to the ground, the omen is for an immediate
funeral; if rather higher in the air, the funeral will
not occur for some time. Corpse candles may be
seen as long before a funeral as three months.

Near the shore at North Ballachulish there used
to be a level spot of grounds, green and grassy,
round which blackthorn bushes grew in something
like a parallelogram form, as if they had been planted
in that way. The spot was always held in terror by
the local folk, who told of strange blue-flame lights
being seen frequently around the place; it was a
place to be avoided at nights. For a long time it was
thought that the place marked the spot on an old
chapel or religious cell. But a later investigation
into old local records proved it to be a small area
of ground set aside in olden times for the burial of
unbaptised infants and suicides.

Father Allan MacDonald, parish priest of Eriskay
at the turn of this century, recorded many aspects
of folklore and traditions of the island of Eriskay
and neighbouring South Uist. In particular, he
recorded many valuable instance of ghostly, or at

least inexplicable, happenings which defied attempts at rationalisation.

Both ghostly lights and sounds feature in his notes. He relates:

' Towards the end of August 1888 I was called to attend a dying woman at South Lochboisdale (South Uist). After administering the rites of religion, a crew and boat were procured. As we were nearing Strom Dearg, one of the rowers drew attention to a light playing on the shore just at the spot where we had embarked. It continued for some time, but its appearance did not cause much astonishment, only we could not imagine what objects any person would have in being in such a spot at such a time. We thought the dying woman would live till morning, but when the boatmen returned home, the woman was dead, and they were told that she was dead just at the time we should have been approaching Strom Dearg. The men spoke of the light and made diligent enquiry if any person had been to the shore, and it was found that no person was there. The coincidence was remarkable.'

Twice in his experience, a carpenter in South Uist, often engaged for the task of making coffins, told of observing ' a lamb surrounded with rays of light standing in the coffin.' These two occurrences took place when the coffin was in a dark part of the house.

Among the noises recorded by Father Allan are those heard at a spot in Eriskay known as *Glaic Charnan an t-Seirm*. These voices were often heard by the island folk at this place and a cairn of stones was set up. The sounds were taken as a *manadh* or warning, foretelling of future events. At one time Eriskay supported a very small population. This was later increased when some of the smaller islands in the Sound of Barra were cleared of crofters, many of whom made their new homes on Eriskay. As Father Allan remarks: ' And there was little wonder that voices should be heard, considering that so many people were to come to stay in the island afterwards.'

About 1870, some boys were playing on a little beach near *Coilleag a' Phrionnsa* (the Prince's Strand, where Prince Charles Edward landed in 1745). It was in the wintertime, with a fine, clear moon shining from a dark sky. After some time, a passing cloud darkened the beach and the boys stopped playing, to rest a while beside a sandhill. Suddenly their dog, which had been previously running about happily chasing the boys' ball, cowered in terror and lay close to the ground. His hair stood erect and he appeared to be in great terror. At the same time as the boys noticed the dog's curious behaviour, they heard a very loud noise, a rumbling and a crashing as though many iron plates were being dragged over the nearby rocks down to the shore. The boys' immediate reaction was to scamper home as fast as they could — which they did, with the dog not far behind them. Father Allan comments that the lads ' were not philosophical enough to examine into possible natural causes for the occurrence.'

Another sound of supernatural origin is associated with Cottertown, near Auchenasie, Keith, Aberdeenshire. It was connected with a murder and is related by Walter Gregor in his book *Folk-lore of the North East of Scotland*:

'On the day on which the deed was done, two men, strangers to the district, called at a farmhouse about three miles from the house in which lived the old folk that were murdered. Shortly before the tragic act was committed, a sound was heard, passing along the road the two men were seen to take, in the direction of the place at which the murder was perpetrated. So loud and extraordinary was the noise that the people left their houses to see what it was that was passing. To the amazement of everyone, nothing was to be seen, though it was moonlight so bright that it aroused attention. All believed something dreadful was to happen, and some proposed to follow the sound. About the time discussion was going on, a blaze of fire arose on the hill of Auchenasie. The foul deed had been accomplished and the cottage set on fire. By the next day we all knew of what the mysterious sound had been the forerunner.'

In Nigg Bay, Easter Ross, there is said to be a sunken village and church. The local tradition was that if anyone heard the sound of the church bell from the sunken spire it foretold a death. Once a boat of fishermen went out into the bay for a spot of quiet fishing. All was peaceful with only the occasional comment between the fishers when one man suddenly looked startled and told his fellows he had just heard bells. With a great speed, the lines were hauled up and the boat was put back into port, all the men believing it to be a death omen for the man who heard the sound. And, indeed, the same man was found drowned three days after the incident.

Early this century, corpse candles or lights were often seen hovering about the Holly Pool, near Taagan, Wester Ross. They were seen for a number of years and only disappeared when two young children were found drowned in the pool, apparently after trying to negotiate it to get to an adjoining harvest field.

One day about eighty years ago, a man stood behind the schoolhouse at Dunmore and looked across West Loch Tarbert in the direction of the ferry plying between Port a' Chaolain, on the Kintyre side of the loch, and Ardpatrick, on the South Knapdale side. As he took in the scene he became aware of a light emerging from the roof of the ferry-house at Port a' Chaolain. It was about seven feet high and was bright enough to be seen at the distance involved, about two and a half miles. The next day the ferryman died.

One ghostly light led to the discovery of a link with a murder which had taken place almost two centuries previously. This occurred on the west coast of Lewis, near the crofting township of Carloway. Local tradition had always related the story of the Irish pedlar who met with his death in a very cruel manner after visiting a house at which he called to ask for directions to get to the next township. The man of the house, thinking that the pedlar would have a well-filled purse, offered to act as a guide. Thanking him for his charity, the pedlar and his guide started off. They had gone only a short distance when the guide turned on the pedlar and cruelly beat him to death. After the killing, the murderer, conscience-stricken, sought to hide the body and the pedlar's goods and purse. The former he buried in soft peaty soil. The latter objects he threw into an old disused well.

In due time, people of the village told each other of the strange light which they saw at nights, and always associated with the same area of ground. For many subsequent generations the light was seen and the story of the pedlar's murder eventually passed into the realm of folktale. But, in 1922, some young men who had themselves often seen the mysterious white light, decided to investigate. One night they followed the light at a comfortable distance and noted carefully the exact spot at which it disappeared. Now, while tradition had always said that the light tended to hover over the old well, in fact the light went out beside it. The men then began to dig around the well and, with an increasing sense of anticipation, found an old and rotten sealskin purse containing a number of Irish pennies. The dates on most of the coins were by then undecipherable, but three bore dates of 1740, 1743 and 1744. Just as strange as the ghost light is the fact that since the coins were uncovered, the light itself has never been seen since.

One night, two farmers were jogging their way

home just outside Stornoway, Lewis. Arriving at a cross-roads, one of the men descended from the horse-drawn trap to make his own way home. Turning round to wave his friend good-night, he noticed that a strange light was hovering in front of the trap. The next day he asked his companion if he had seen the light. Indeed, the man had, and in fact had whipped up his pony in an effort to catch up with it. Two days later a farmer was drowned in Stornoway harbour. And his body was carried home in the same trap as the two companions had used only two days before.

In the island of Luing another light was once seen, this time by a man who followed the bright shape until it vanished over a rough-stone bridge, which was crudely made but was strong enough to carry the weight of a horse and loaded cart. He related the incident to his neighbours, who could give no explanation, except that it was obviously some kind of omen. The following morning, the son of a local farmer was returning home on the horse he had just shod at the local smithy. No more than half way across, the bridge suddenly collapsed and rider and mount were thrown into the stream. The horse fell on the rider and its weight pinned him under. He was drowned.

The island of Benbecula is noted for its angling, particularly the trout which abound in its many lochs. During the summer of 1938 a strange light was seen hovering over Loch Olavant; this light persisted for several consecutive days. Those who saw it were convinced that it was a portent of some

kind. On the day following the last appearance of
the light, an angler, not an islander, who had for
many years favoured angling holidays on Benbecula,
had a heart seizure while he was investigating a
tiny island in the loch for birds' nests. The light
was described as ' a glowing fire like a smouldering
peat on the little island . . . and there was nothing
to account for it.'

There are many sites of shielings in the Outer
Hebrides and, being remote from inhabited town-
ships, they are associated with tales of wonder and
horror. Most of these are legends and folktales. But
there are some of less doubtful origin. One story
tells of a mysterious light which was seen persistently
for about half a century near Leuchan, in Harris.
As late as 1944 it was seen by several people who,
thinking it was a signal of some kind, hurried to
the spot. But when they arrived at the place, the
light had disappeared. Marsh gas has been suggested
but the local folk put a different interpretation on
the light.

Another light is still seen in the township of
Manish, also in Harris. The light has been observed
by many people, always above a particular house.
The real mystery surrounding this particular light
is not so much in the light itself but in the fact that
there is nothing unusual either about the site of the
house or the history of the building.

In 1949 two friends were enjoying a pleasant
evening together close by Loch Duntelchaig, a few
miles from Inverness. As the dusk pressed in on
them, they went into their car to finish off their

conversation and their sandwiches. As they talked they became aware of a strange light hovering about ten feet in front of the car bonnet. One of the men turned the switch for the car headlamps, thinking he had left them on. But in fact the lamps were off. The light persisted for some time before it slowly faded away. Puzzled, the men got out to investigate, but found absolutely nothing.

On the west coast of the island of Barra, Outer Hebrides, two elderly sisters were preparing for bed after an extremely hard day in their small village store. One of the sisters was deaf, so much so that even a gun-shot made little impression. By the time they had made up their accounts, and saw to the ordering of more stores it was nearly two a.m. They tumbled into bed with the prospect of a good and full night's sleep in front of them. Towards the early hours of the morning, both sisters sat up in bed, startled, and the deaf one asked what was the terrible noise she had heard. Or had she only dreamt it? Her sister, thinking to comfort her, said it was only rats, though, ' I knew fine it was a loud knock on the window pane. I went and undid the door and felt with my hands round the house, it being very dark. There was nothing and nobody, and the night was dead silent, not even the sea making a murmur. So I went back to bed and to sleep. The next night, and it was at the very same time, we were wakened again by the loud knock, a ringing hard knock on the window so that you would wonder that it did not break the glass. And she (the deaf one) heard it the same as me. I rose again, but there was no one there. The third night I lay awake for I kenned fine I was needed. It came at the same time once more, and this time the deaf one did *not* hear. A soft, quiet knock on the pane and up I got and out. And there, crouching beside the window, was Sandy MacLean, sobbing like to break his heart.'

The lad had come to the store for the winding sheet for his mother who had just died.

At the turn of the century in Tiree, an old woman lay on her death-bed and while the rest of the household sat up with her, the youngest member, a lad, was packed off to his bed. Through the night he heard what he took to be the trampling of dogs in a loft above his sleeping place, and this he heard so distinctly that he asked his father next day what made him put the dogs there. The answer he got was that there were no dogs in the loft. The lad also heard a plank sliding down from the loft and striking on end in the passage between the doors. The following night the old woman died, and the lad himself was sent up to the loft to bring down planks to make her coffin. A plank slipped from his hands and, falling on its end in the passage, made exactly the same noise as he had heard the night before.

About 1860 the trampling of horses and the rattling of a conveyance were heard after dark, coming up to the farmhouse of Liaran in Rannoch. Every person in the house thought a conveyance of some kind was really there. The horses were distinctly heard turning round in the courtyard. On looking out nothing was to be seen or heard. Four or five days after, a hearse (a kind of conveyance until then unknown in that part of Scotland) came from Appin with the remains of a cousin of the Liaran family who had been suddenly killed by a kick from a horse.

As late as 1867 a coach was seen proceeding silently through the streets of a village in Ayrshire going in the direction of a burying-ground, and was believed by the village folk to be that of a rich lady in the neighbourhood known as Brimstone Betty, who died shortly after the sighting, not in the odour of sanctity.

In one house in Appin, Argyll, noises were heard coming from a cupboard in a room, as though someone was fumbling among the bottles of wine and liquor kept there. The noises were heard by several people before the sudden death of a member of the family. After the funeral, the returning burial party were offered hospitality from bottles which had been stored in that same cupboard.

5

STRANGE HAPPENINGS

FOR every person who has genuinely seen a ghost, there are many more who have been witness to some strange occurrence which has defied rational explanation. Mysterious happenings include divination of death, the hearing of voices, seeing ghostly armies and so on, all of which tend to add credence to the existence of another world operating on a fluctuating time-scale and contemporaneously with our own rather time-fixed world.

South of Inverness there is a chain of attractive lochs which are harnessed to provide the town of Inverness with its water supply. One of these lochs is Loch Ashie. Close by are several cairns and tumuli and a large boulder (at the loch's north-western end) popularly known as King Fingal's Seat. It is said that a battle once took place on the moor in the immediate vicinity, between Fionn, or Fingal, and the men of Lochlann (Norway) who were led by their leader, King Ashie. Tradition has it, and a number of people living now have confirmed the tradition, that soon after dawn on May Day a ghostly battle is seen in progress between the two factions.

At the beginning of the 1870s, the battle was clearly observed by several people. It was thought at the time to be a trick of light which projected onto the Inverness moor a mirage of men fighting in a battle in the then progressing Franco-Prussian War. But as the images were seen after that war had ended, people sought to look for other explanations. During the First World War a cyclist in the area met up with three men walking along in front of him. To

Portree, Isle of Skye

his amazement, he cycled right through them, and when he turned round he was even more amazed to see the traditional phantom armies in close formation fighting for their lives.

Another ghostly battle has been seen in Glen

Shiel. The original was fought in 1719 between the King's troops under General Wightman and a force of Spaniards who had landed in the west to help the Old Chevalier. The King's troops were victorious. On suitable nights the battle has been re-enacted with ghostly men, not only fighting, but beating a weary retreat up the Pass, and men on both sides silently burying their dead.

The bloody deeds of a nation's history burn deep into the mind and remain as fresh as though they were yesterday's occurrences. This is the case with the Forty-Five: the battlefield at Culloden sees over a hundred thousand visitors each year, many of whom are Scots and expatriate Highlanders who pay a kind of pilgrimage to the scene which sparked off a trail of death, disaster and humiliation for the Highlanders and their kith and kin. One story of the Forty-Five centres round a well on the road from Uig to Portree. It is known locally as Prince Charlie's Well. On the 15th of April 1746 the ghost of a tall young man was seen in its vicinity, with a sad and mournful expression on his face, and muttering in a voice that was heard by some people: 'Defeated, defeated, defeated.' The ghost then vanished from sight and the whole thing was taken as an omen of disaster. Suddenly, and without any warning at all, a ghost army was seen with arms clashing and drums beating. This sight also vanished. On the following day, the 16th of April, 1746, the Battle of Culloden was fought, and the forces of the Prince were defeated and scattered over the whole of the Highlands. Shortly afterwards, the fugitive Prince himself slaked his thirst at that same well. This was one of the many incidents recorded in the Highlands when coming events were foretold by the sighting of sad shadows.

The sighting of ghostly armies is not at all uncommon and often the phantom warriors are seen by a number of people at the same time, perhaps proving that it is not one particular individual's over-generous imagination working overtime. One of the most outstanding authenticated accounts of such a sighting is contained in a letter to *The Times* in 1926. The original, in the narrator's handwriting, still exists. The text of the letter is as follows:

'Letter from Mr. Bell, Writer to the Signet, Inverary, to Colonel Campbell, Yr., of Shawfield.

'Sir, — As you wish to have an account of the vision which my father and grandfather saw in the neighbourhood of this place (Inverary), I will endeavour to comply with your request. I have heard of it with all its circumstances so often related by them both, when together, as well as by my father separately, since my grandfather's decease, that I am as fully convinced they saw the vision as if I had seen it myself. At the same time I must acknowledge that, however desirous I am to oblige Lady Charlotte and you, I commit the account of it to writing with some degree of reluctance, well knowing how little reliance is given by the more intelligent classes of people to a narration of that kind, and how little it corresponds with the ordinary course of causes and effects.

'This vision was seen by them both about 3

o'clock afternoon of a very clear sunny day in the months of June or July between the years 1746 and 1753. I cannot go nearer to ascertain the year.

'My grandfather was then a farmer in Glenary, which you know is within four miles of this place, and my father, who was at that time a young unmarried man, resided in family with him. On the morning of the day above mentioned, my grandfather, having occasion to transact some business in Glenshiray, took my father along with him. They went there by crossing the hill which separates it from Glenary, and, their business in Glenshiray being finished, a little after midday they came round by Inverary in order to return home. At that time the road generally used from Glenshiray to Inverary lay upon the west side of the River of Shiray, all the way to Garran Bridge, when it joined the high road which leads from Inverary to the low country by that bridge.

'As soon as they came to that bridge and had turned towards Inverary, up the high road, being then as you know within sight of a part of the old town of Inverary which has since been demolished — the ground upon which the new town presently stands and of the whole line of road leading from it to the above mentioned bridge — they were very much surprised to behold a great number of men under arms marching on foot towards them. At this time the foremost ranks were only advanced as far as Kilmalieu (the burying ground); they were marching in regular order and as closely as they could move, from the point of the new town near the quay where Captain Gillie's house now stands, along the shore and high road, and crossing the river of Aray near the town, at or about the spot where the new bridge has since been built. Of the rear there appeared to be no end; the ground upon which the new town now stands was then surrounded by a park wall, and the road beyond it lay in a circular direction between that wall and the sea. From the nature of the ground my father and grandfather could see no further than the wall, and as the army was advancing in front, the rear as regularly succeeded and advanced from the farthest verge of their view.

'This extraordinary sight, which was wholly unexpected, so much attracted their attention that they stood a considerable time to observe it. They then walked slowly on, but stopped now and then, with their eyes constantly fixed on the objects before them. Meantime the army continuing regularly to advance, they counted that it had 15 or 16 pairs of colours, and they observed that the men nearest to them were marching upon the road six or seven abreast, or in each line, attended by a number of women and children, both above and below the road, some of whom were carrying tin cans and other implements of cookery, which I am told is customary upon a march. They were clothed in red (but as to this particular circumstance I do not recollect whether my grandfather mentioned it or not, though I know my father did), and the sun shone so bright that the gleam of their arms, consisting of muskets and bayonets, dazzled their sight; they also observed, between Kilmalieu and the Salmon draught, an animal resembling a deer or a horse in the middle of a crowd of soldiers who, as they conjectured, were stabbing it or spurring it on with their bayonets.

' My father, who had never seen an army before, naturally put a number of questions to my grandfather (who had served with the Argyllshire Highlanders in assisting to suppress the Rebellion in 1745) concerning the probable route and destination of the army which was now advancing towards them, and the number of which it seemed to consist. My grandfather replied that he supposed that it had come from Ireland and had landed in Kintyre, and that it was proceeding to England, and that in his opinion it was more numerous than the armies on both sides at the battle of Culloden.

' My father having particularly remarked that the rear ranks were continually running forward in order to overtake those who were before them, and inquiring into the reason of that circumstance, my grandfather told him that that was always the case with the rear — that the least obstacle stopped and threw them behind, which necessarily, and in a still greater degree, retarded the march of those who were behind them, and obliged them to run forward till they gained their own places again, and he therefore advised my father if ever he went into the army, to endeavour if possible to get into the front rank, which always marched with leisure and ease, whilst those in the rear were generally kept running in the manner he had seen.

' My father and grandfather were now come to

the thorn bush between Garran bridge and the gate
of the Deer Park, and at the same time the van of
the army had advanced very near to that gate, which
you know is but a very short distance (I believe not
above 150 or 200 yards from the thorn bush) and,
as the road forms into a (right-angled) corner at that
gate, and the front of the army being then directly
opposite to them, they had of course, a better opportunity of observing it minutely than they had at
first done. The vanguard, they then observed, consisted of a party of 40 or 50 men, preceded by an
officer on foot; at a little distance behind them
another officer appeared riding upon a grey dragoon
horse; he was the only person they observed on
horseback, and from his appearance and station in
the march they considered him as the Commander-
in-Chief. He had on a gold laced hat, and a blue
hussar cloak, with wide open loose sleeves, all lined
with red; he also wore boots and spurs; the rest of
his dress they could not see. My father took such
particular notice of him that he often declared he
would have known him perfectly well if he had ever
seen him again. Behind this officer the rest of the
army marched all in one body as far as they observed,
but attended by women and children, as I mentioned
above.

'My father's curiosity being now sufficiently
gratified, he thought it was high time to provide for
his own security. He represented to my grandfather
that it was very probable that these men who were
advancing towards them would force them to go
along with them, or use them otherwise ill, and he

therefore proposed that they should both go out of their way, by climbing over the stone dyke which fences the deer park from the high road, observing that the spot where they then were was very convenient for that purpose as the thorn bush would help to screen them from their view while going over the dyke. To this my grandfather objected, saying that as he was a middle-aged man, and had seen some service, he did not believe they would give any trouble to him, but he told my father as he was a young man and that they might probably take him along with them, he might go out of their way or not, as he thought fit.

' Upon this my father leapt instantly over the dyke; he then walked behind it for a little time in the direction of the Garran bridge, and when he had got about halfway he turned up towards the clumps in the neighbourhood of the bridge, believing that he was then out of the reach of pursuit, should any be attempted. But when he arrived near the clumps, he looked back to observe the motions of the army, and whether any person attempted to follow him, but he found to his astonishment that they were all vanished, not a soul of them was to be seen! As soon as he recovered from the surprise which this extraordinary scene had occasioned him, he returned to my grandfather, and cried out, " What has become of the men? " My grandfather, who seems not to have paid much attention to them after my father left him, then observing that they had all disappeared, answered with an equal degree of astonishment that he could not tell.

' As they proceeded on their way to Inverary, he recommended to my father to keep what they had seen a profound secret, adding that they would make themselves ridiculous by mentioning it, for that no person would believe they had seen a vision so extraordinary; at the same time, he told him that though he (my grandfather) might not live to see it, my father might probably live to see the vision realised. This conversation was scarcely ended, when they met one Stewart, an old man, who then resided in Glenshiray, going home and driving a horse before him. This, as they believed, was the same animal they had observed before, surrounded by a crowd. My father, notwithstanding the admonitions he had received, was not able to contain himself. He asked Stewart " What had become of the people who had been travelling with him? " Stewart, not understanding the drift of the question, answered that nobody had been in company with him since he left Inverary, but that he had never travelled on so warm a day, that the air was so close and sultry he was hardly able to breathe, and that his horse had become so weak and feeble that he was obliged to alight and drive him before him.

' The account I now send you of this vision was not only communicated by my father and grandfather to me, but was also communicated by them to many others in this place and neighbourhood soon after it happened, it being scarcely possible that so extraordinary an occurrence should be long concealed. It is, no doubt, extremely difficult to account for it upon the ordinary principles which regulate

human events, but no person acquainted with my
father and grandfather ever supposed that either of
them was capable of inventing such a story, and
accordingly, as far as I can understand, no person
to whom they told it ever doubted that they told
anything but the truth.

' My grandfather died several years ago; my father
only died within these two years, but neither of them
saw their vision realised, although, indeed, my
father had strong expectations of seeing it a few
years before his death, particularly at the time of
the Irish Rebellion and of the last threatened
invasion by the French. It may perhaps be not
improper to add that upon the day on which the
vision was seen neither my father nor grandfather
had tasted anything stronger than milk, so that
whatever was the cause of the impression made upon
their imaginations, it could not be owing to any
intemperance.

' I shall be extremely happy if this little story can
contribute in any degree to your own or Lady
Charlotte's amusement, and am, with due respect,
Sir,

Your most obedient servant,
ARCHIBALD BELL.

Inverary, Nov. 8, 1808.'

As recently as 1956, two young men were engaged
on a geological survey of the Isle of Skye. They spent
one particular night under canvas at Harta Corrie.
At about two o'clock in the morning, one of them
woke, rose to throw back the tent flap and stepped

outside. ' I was astonished to see groups of kilted men. There must have been dozens of them. They were scrambling along the mountain-side on the other side of a small burn.' The noiselessness of the men's movements struck him as so strange. All was quiet. He woke his companion and both of them watched for about eight minutes while the shadowy figures flitted about in the heather. Later they learned that in the same corrie is the Bloody Stone, a boulder which marks the scene of a desperate fight between the MacDonalds and the MacLeods in 1395.

The following is the personal experience of a friend of the writer's, Ronald MacDonald Douglas, who, at the time, was living in a croft house near Inverness:

' On many an occasion, since coming to live in this there being anyone playing within at least a couple of miles. Making enquiries, I discovered that, as a matter of fact, there was not a piper within six or seven miles; and, more than that, I found that there could not possibly be anyone piping for far more miles than that in the direction from which I was always hearing the sounds of music coming; and, still more than that, I discovered that the man who had occupied this croft for years before I came to it, had heard the piping regularly, but no one had believed him.

' Anyhow, the piping came to me at irregular intervals — and not always after dark — for that matter, I heard it as recently as two days ago. At first, I tried to find some other reason for the sounds. Was it the wind in the trees? Was it the wind playing over and through the cairns with which the moor is dotted? Was it, even, the wind rippling over the house, I have heard the sound of pipes being played — and far and away, and distant was their tone — and strange, too, was something else about them. At first, the strange tone baffled me — there was something missing — but, at last, I discovered what it was. The pipes I was hearing had the tone of the pipes I had often heard played in Ireland, the kind of pipes that were played, as far as I can gather, in Scotland two or three centuries ago (the pipes with the two drones instead of the usual modern Scottish three).

' But the fact that the heavy droning was not to be heard might, I thought, have been accounted for by distance. There was, I knew, no possibility of listened for a few minutes and then went in to bed.

' I lay awake for a long time, and then I must have dozed. But, suddenly, I sat up. The moonlight was streaming in across my bed; and outside, but distantly, there was going on the most infernal and unearthly din I have ever heard. There was the clash of metal on metal, and the hoarse yellings of men. Over all the din there was repeated time and time again some particular phrase that I could not distinguish; and, over and above everything, over all the clashing and all the yelling, there was the wild high skirl of the pipes, and not the pipes of iron roof of the barn, or playing in and around the broken timbers at the end of the steading?

' It was not any one of these things, for the sounds came from a far greater distance . . .

' And now comes the real story, for the tale of the phantom piper is no more than a preliminary to the big affair.

' One brilliantly moonlit night at the beginning of this year (1935) I had sat writing until midnight. Then, before going to bed, I went for a stroll over the moor. There was not a cloud in the sky, nor even a drift of mist about the hill-tops. Every tree on the moor stood out — each like a black silhouette — and clearly there came to me the sounds of the burn waters thrashing down the gully.

' When suddenly, from the ridge of the other side, there came to me, high and clear, the sounds of the *piobaireachd*. But I had grown so accustomed to hearing the strange pipes that I no more than one lone piper, but the pipes of surely no less than half a dozen.

' Now, I have done my share of fighting, but never in all my life have I known such ghastly fear as was on me that night, lying there in my own bed, with four good thick stone walls around me. I was forced from my bed. I had to go. And there was no heroism in it. I was scared stiff.

' And then I flung my kilt about me. As I went down the stairs, it was a great soldier that went down — hair on end and trembling in every limb!

' Then the sounds stopped. And then began again — but with a difference; there was still the clatter of metals, but the clatter was the clatter of hanging accoutrements, and not the clash of arms in action. And the sounds were coming nearer. Down one side of the burn they came, and up the other, and over

the moor and across the heather and bog; the sounds
of marching men, but all unreal, something like the
sounds of surf beating on a distant shore were the
sounds that the feet of the host appeared to be
making. And the strange yelling had changed from
the yells of men in fight to the triumphant and
derisive yells of men who had been victorious. And,
over it all, was the ranting skirling of the pipers.

'By this time I could hear the dogs whining in
the part of the steading where they sleep. I managed
to run to let them out; there are three of them —
an extremely sagacious young bitch, and her two
sons, a couple of hefty young lads about five months
old. They dashed out of the steading, all three of
them, in the direction from which the sounds were
coming, barking and howling for all they were
worth. Then they came tearing back. The bitch lay
down at my feet, whining in a way I had never heard
before, but the two pups streaked away across the
moor in the opposite direction like a couple of
greyhounds.

'Nearer and nearer came the marching ghost-
army. I could hear everything, but I could see
nothing. The moor, to the eyes, appeared as deserted
as ever. I stood petrified by the barn door.

'The cohort passed within a few yards of me —
first the pipers, and then a long straggle of talking,
yelling men — and amongst it all there was the
occasional screaming of a woman!

'Then the army, or whatever it was, with the
pipers leading, *passed clean through the house,* and
went off south-westerly. I heard the passing. I waited,

and gradually the sounds grew fainter. The ghost-army faded away into the night.

' There is no more to tell, except that the hill on the other side of the burn, the hill from which the sounds of the fighting had first come, is known as *Mam a' Chatha* (the Hill of the Battle).'

The Battle of Killiecrankie is as famous an episode in Scottish history as any other and the Pass is no doubt full of spiritual associations which are given only to the more sensitive to ' see.' Phantom soldiers are commonly seen in the Pass and one such sighting has been recorded. It took place in the latter years of the last century:

' The incident I am about to relate took place in the autumn. I was on a cycle tour in Scotland and, making Pitlochry my temporary headquarters, rode over one evening to view the historic Pass of Killie-crankie. It was late when I arrived there. I was so entranced at the view that I perched myself on a rock at the foot of one of the great cliffs that form the walls of the Pass, and, throwing my head back, imagined myself in fairyland. I paid no heed to time, nor did I think of stirring, until the dark shadows of the night fell across my face. I then started up in a panic, and was about to pedal off in hot haste when a strange notion suddenly seized me. I had a latchkey, plenty of sandwiches, a warm cape, why should I not camp out there till early morning.

' Selecting the most comfortable-looking boulder I could see, I scrambled on to the top of it, and, with my cloak drawn tightly over my back and shoulders, commenced my vigil. The cold mountain air, sweet with the perfume of gorse and heather, intoxicated me, and I gradually sank into a heavenly torpor, from which I was abruptly aroused by a dull boom, that I at once associated with distant musketry. All was then still, still as the grave, and, on glancing at the watch I wore strapped on my wrist, I saw it was two o'clock. A species of nervous dread now laid hold of me, and a thousand and one vague fancies, all the more distressing because of their vagueness, oppressed and disconcerted me. Moreover, I was impressed for the first time with the extraordinary solitude — solitude that seemed to belong to a period far other than the present, and, as I glanced at the solitary pines and boulders, I more than half expected to see the wild, ferocious face of some robber chief peering at me from behind them.

' This feeling at length became so acute that, in a panic of fear, ridiculous, puerile fear, I forcibly withdraw my gaze and concentrated it abstractedly on the ground at my feet. I then listened, and in the rustling of a leaf, the humming of some night insect, the whizzing of a bat, the whispering of the wind as it moaned softly past me, I fancied I detected something that was not ordinary.

' I blew my nose, and had barely ceased marvelling at the loudness of its reverberations before the piercing, ghoulish shriek of an owl sent the blood in torrents to my heart. Then there came again the queer booming noise I had heard before, but which I could now no longer doubt was the report of firearms. I looked in the direction of the sound and my heart almost stopped. Racing towards me, as if not merely for his life, but his soul, came the figure of a Highlander. The wind rustling through his long, dishevelled hair blew it completely over his forehead, narrowly missing his eyes, which were fixed ahead of him in a ghastly, agonised stare. He had not a vestige of colour and, in the powerful glow of the moonbeams, his skin shone livid. He ran with huge bounds, and, what added to my terror and made me doubly aware he was nothing mortal, was that each time his feet struck the hard, smooth road, upon which I could well see there was no sign of a stone, there came the sound, the unmistakeable sound, of the scattering of gravel.

' On, on he came, with cyclonic swiftness; his bare sweating elbows pressed into his panting sides; his great, dirty, coarse, hairy fists screwed up in bony bunches in front of him; the foam-flakes thick on his clenched, grinning lips; the blood-drops oozing down his sweating thighs.

' It was all real, infernally, hideously real, even to the most minute details: the flying up and down of his kilt, sporran, and swordless scabbard; the bursting of the seam of his coat, near the shoulder; and the absence of one of his clumsy shoe-buckles. I tried hard to shut my eyes, but was compelled to keep them open, and follow his every movement as, darting past me, he left the roadways, and, leaping several of the smaller obstacles that barred his way, finally disappeared behind some of the bigger boulders. I then heard the loud rat-rat of drums, accompanied by the shrill voices of fifes and flutes, and at the farther end of the Pass, their arms glittering brightly in the silvery moonbeams, appeared a regiment of scarlet-clad soldiers. At the head rode a mounted officer, after him came the band, and then, four abreast, a long line of warriors; in their centre two ensigns, and, on their flanks, officers and non-commissioned officers with swords and pikes; more mounted men bringing up the rear.

' On they came, the fifes and flutes ringing out with a weird clearness in the hushed mountain air. I could hear the ground vibrate, the gravel crunch and scatter, as they steadily and mechanically advanced; tall men, enormously tall men, with set, white faces and livid eyes. Every instant I expected they would see me, and I became sick with terror at the thought of meeting all those pale, flashing eyes.

' But from this I was happily saved; no one appeared to notice me, and they all passed by me without so much as a twist or turn of the head, their feet keeping time to one everlasting and monotonous tramp, tramp, tramp. I got up and watched until the last of them had turned the bend of the Pass, and the sheen of his weapons and trappings could no longer be seen; then I remounted my boulder and wondered if anything further would happen. It was now half-past two.

' Then, confronting me, on the opposite side of the road, was a tree, an ash, and, to my surprise, despite the fact that the breeze had fallen and there was scarcely a breath of wind, the tree swayed violently to and fro, whilst there proceeded from it the most dreadful moanings and groanings. I was so terrified that I caught hold of my bicycle and tried to mount, but I was obliged to desist as I had not a particle of strength in my limbs. Then, to assure myself that the moving of the tree was not an illusion, I rubbed my eyes, pinched myself, called aloud; but it made no difference — the rustling, bending, and tossing still continued.

' Summoning up courage, I stepped into the road to get a closer view, when to my horror my feet kicked against something, and, on looking down, I perceived the body of an English soldier, with a ghastly wound in his chest. I gazed around, and there, on all sides of me, from one end of the valley to the other, lay dozens of bodies. The bodies of men and horses; Highlanders and English, white-checked, lurid eyes, and bloody-browed. It was a hotch-potch of livid, gory awfulness. Here was the writhing, wriggling figure of an officer with half his face shot away; and there, a horse with no head; and there — but I cannot dwell on such horrors, the very memory of which makes me feel sick and faint. The air, that beautiful fresh mountain air, resounded with their moanings and groanings, and reeked with the smell of their blood.

' As I stood rooted to the ground with horror, not knowing which way to look or turn, I suddenly saw drop from the ash, the form of a woman, a Highland girl, with bold, handsome features, raven black hair, and the whitest of arms and feet. In one hand she carried a wicker basket, in the other a knife, a broad-bladed, sharp-edged, horn-handled knife. A gleam of avarice and cruelty came into her large dark eyes, as, wandering around her, they rested on the rich facings of the English officers' uniforms.

'I knew what was in her mind, forgetting that she was but a ghost and that they were all ghosts, I moved heaven and earth to stop her. I could not. Making straight for a wounded officer that lay moaning piteously on the ground, some ten feet away from me, she spurned with her slender, graceful feet, the bodies of the dead and dying English that came in her way. Then, snatching the officer's sword and pistol from him, she knelt down, and, with a look of devilish glee in her glorious eyes, calmly plunged her knife into his heart, working the blade backwards and forwards to assure herself she had made a thorough job of it. Anything more hellish I could not have imagined, and yet it fascinated me. Her act of cruelty over, she spoiled her victim of his rings, epaulets, buttons and gold lacings, and, having placed them in her basket, proceeded elsewhere. In some cases, unable to move the rings easily, she chopped off the fingers, and popped them, just as they were, into her basket. Neither was her mode of dispatch always the same, for while she put some men out of their misery in the manner I have described, she cut the throats of others, whilst others again she settled with the butt-ends of their guns or pistols. In all she murdered a full half-score, and was decamping with her booty when her gloating eyes suddenly encountered mine, and with a shrill scream of rage she rushed towards me.

' I was an easy victim, for strain and pray how I would, I could not move an inch. Raising her flashing blade high above her head, an expression of fiendish glee in her staring eyes, she made ready to strike me. This was the climax. My overstrained nerves could stand no more, and ere the blow had time to descend, I pitched heavily forward and fell at her feet. When I recovered, every phantom had vanished, and the Pass glowed with all the cheerful freshness of the early morning sun. Not a whit the worse for my adventure, I cycled swiftly home, and ate as only one can eat who has spent the night amid the banks and braes of bonnie Scotland.'

Near the little picturesque village of Dores, on the eastern side of Loch Ness, there is the Well of the Phantom Hand. This is said to be the home of an extra-large spirit whose outstretched hand is sometimes to be seen reaching out over the heads of those about to drink from the well's waters. Many thirsty travellers have been terrified of the sight, but remained unharmed. The well has been associated with this tradition for the past two hundred years.

Many years ago in South Uist there was a house in which lived a family with a girl of seven who was dumb from birth. One night the old man in the house died and, pending the funeral arrangements, the corpse was laid on a suitable broad plank of wood. His son, the girl's father, left the house in the care of his wife and daughter while he went in search of a priest. He had not been gone long when suddenly the girl, who had never spoken a word in her life, said, '*Tha mo sheanair ag eirigh*' (my grandfather is rising).

Startled, the mother replied, 'If these are your first words of speech it is like we were not here,' and she took herself and the child into a small back room and barricaded the door with two heavy quern-stones and other suitable articles.

Not before time, it seemed, for the corpse rose from its plank and tried to push the room door open. Finding this impossible, it then began to dig under the doorpost with its nails. It was almost half-way through when the cock crew and the corpse stiffened. It was found in this position when the son returned.

The body was immediately placed in a coffin and was found to be extraordinarily heavy. The weight was so great that it put a severe strain on those who were carrying the bier. Then, not far from the graveyard, the weight suddenly lifted and the coffin became obviously the container of an ordinary corpse. This incident is supposed to have occurred at the latter end of the 18th century and is still told in South Uist.

It is often said that one of the most common reasons for a ghost's appearance is an attempt to right certain things which were left undone in life, or else to repay some kind of debt that might have been in the mind at the moment of death. In the Proceedings of the Psychical Society there is the story of a priest who reports as follows:

'In July 1838 I left Edinburgh to take charge of the Perthshire missions. On my arrival in Perth I was called on by a Presbyterian woman, Anne

Simpson, who for more than a week had been in the utmost anxiety to see a priest. This woman stated that a woman lately dead, named Moloy, slightly known to Anne Simpson, had appeared to her during the night for several nights, urging her to go to the priest, who would pay a sum of money, three and tenpence, which the deceased owed to a person not specified.

Culloden Moor

'I made enquiries, and found that a woman of that name had died and who had acted as washerwoman and followed the regiment. Following up the inquiry, I found a grocer with whom she had dealt, and on asking him if a female named Moloy owed him anything, he turned up his books and told me that she did owe him three and tenpence.

I paid the sum. Subsequently the Presbyterian woman came to me, saying that she was no more troubled.'

That bonny fechter for Scotland, Miss Wendy Wood, tells of an unusual experience she once had at Culloden Battlefield. The redolent atmosphere is not so apparent in the summer, however, when the grounds are swarming with visitors; but rather in the winter months, when few people are around, and the battlefield and grave grounds take on their sad, sombre and reflective character again till the next tourist season comes round.

Miss Wood tells of the time when she and a party of Scottish patriots visited Culloden to look around the area. Many years previous to this particular visit Miss Wood had been at Culloden and, in the course of that tour, had gone to the Well of the Dead. Leaning over the well she saw, not her own reflection in the water, but that of a man with a drawn face, wild eyes and long black hair. Now, on this much later occasion, she performed much the same action. Leaning over the well, she gazed into the water's surface — and was confronted with the reflection of the same man. His eyes were filled with an agony of pain from a brutal and open cut which ran across his brow. Blood clotted the hair and, as she looked, Miss Wood also experienced a pain in her brow. With great difficulty she managed to tear herself away from the well and returned to her friends, trying to hide her distress at what she had seen. But her appearance was noticed by her friends, who made an effort to comfort her. Miss

Wood records that it took her three days to recover from the experience, and a further four days before the pain in her brow, over her left eye, subsided.

Miss Wood also relates in her autobiography *Yours Sincerely for Scotland* the instance of a neighbour who had looked in on her to say goodbye before he went off to serve in the Mercantile Marine. As Miss Wood looked at him she saw water pouring over him. This is a familiar omen of a coming drowning. The writer's grandmother had many such 'sights' connected with her immediate family. After the man had gone, Miss Wood mentioned what she had seen to another person. Later, she heard that the sailor had reached America safely and Miss Wood tried to convince herself that his arrival was a good omen. Then came a wire to say that he had landed in Hull and was hoping to be home the following day. But, instead of the sailor, another wire arrived to say that in the previous night of bombing he had been thrown from the gangway of his ship and drowned.

A woman in the Western Isles was walking down the township road one evening when she was suddenly struck by some unidentifiable object and thrown to the ground. She searched around, but could not find anything to explain the occurrence, and casually put it down to the supernatural. A few days afterwards, a neighbour died and a general request was put out for planks of wood to make a suitable coffin. The woman gave some and thought it less than strange that the lads who had come for the planks threw all their collected wood down at the very place where she had been thrown to the ground, to start the making of the coffin.

Another story is told about a plank of wood in South Uist. Some children, in the presence of three men, one of whom was a minister, were playing nearby using a large plank of wood as a slide. Suddenly, and without warning, the plank gave out a loud moaning sound which so terrified the children that they ran away. A few days later the same plank was taken up to be used in the making of a coffin.

One night in South Uist a woman was busy carding wool when she caught sight of a ' candle ' of light pass by her to the upper end of the house where a boy in rather delicate health was lying in bed. Thinking that this omen indicated that something was about to happen to the lad, she called out, and got a reply from him saying that he was quite fit and well. The next day, a young man who had called at the woman's house to collect some jars for whisky to serve at his brother's funeral was discovered to be missing. This young man, it seemed, had passed by the woman's house on the way to do some fishing. He was later found dead at the side of a stream.

As might be expected, the island of Iona figures in many stories of strange sightings and experiences. Inside the Abbey itself, ghostly chanting of monks has been heard, and the monks themselves, or, rather, their centuries-old spirits, have been seen in slow procession in the vicinity of the Abbey. One woman has recorded her sighting of a monk: ' I saw him clearly with mental vision — so vividly that I'd

know him at once if I saw him again. Very gentle
and benign he was. He wore a brownish robe, and a
hempen rope round his waist; and there was a halo
round his head.'

Iona

On another occasion, a man was walking over a
part of the island which he knew like the back of
his hand. As he walked, however, he became slowly
aware that the scene before his eyes was strange and
one which he failed to recognise. In a growing state
of confusion he walked over to the White Sands.
No sooner had he arrived when he noticed a fleet
of Viking longboats emerge from behind a small
islet, *Eilean Annraidh,* 'fourteen long, thin boats

with high stems.' As he continued to look at this uncanny sight, he saw the boats land on the shore. Out of these leapt armed men who fell on a group of monks nearby. These they quickly dispatched before making off in the direction of the Abbey. Shortly afterwards, still seeming to be fixed in a time long past, the onlooker saw the returning men loaded with booty boarding their ships and push off from the White Sands.

As his time-slip brought him back to his own time and hour he found he could recall some of the emblems which he had seen emblazoned on the longboats' square sails. These were later verified by authorities as belonging to the late tenth century.

Another person who was witness to a similar occurrence on Iona was the late F. C. B. Cadell, the Scottish artist. A year or so before he died in 1938 he was painting near the Hermit's Cell when he found himself surrounded by fighting men of an obvious ghostly nature. The vision so disturbed him that he packed up his easel and paints and left the spot. He recorded later that he was puzzled by the fact that the knees of the warriors were on the level of the ground. This point could be explained in that during the intervening centuries the ground level might well have risen a foot or so.

A hooded maiden has often been seen on Loch Craignish, in the valley of the River Barbreck, between Ardfern and Ford. She is reported as having long hair which surrounds a very pale face. She is usually seen sitting on a rock dressed in an unspecified tartan. A hood hides most of her features. Her significance or import has never been discovered.

Abbotsford

The home of Sir Walter Scott during the last twenty years of his life was his beloved Abbotsford. He was very interested in all forms of the occult and anything unusual and mysterious attracted him. One of his own personal experiences he duly recorded. This took place in the year of 1818, during some alterations in the building. Sir Walter remarked on a 'violent noise, like drawing heavy boards along the new part of the house.' The following night, at about 2 a.m., the same noises were heard again. Sir Walter investigated, accompanied by " Beardie's Broadsword," but was never able to discover the reason for the noises. At that time, however, the agent who was responsible for the alterations at Abbotsford died suddenly. The incident of the noises and the untimely death cannot but seem to be connected in some way.

Towards the latter end of the last century, a number of people on Eriskay were startled to hear coming from the direction of nearby Lingay Island cries as though a boatful of people were in sore distress. The cries were so real that a boat was immediately put out from Eriskay. After this boat had gone for some time, the cries stopped. The boat slowed down and those in her listened in silence. But nothing was heard. The crew were on the point of returning to land when the noises started once more. The craft was turned round and made off in the general direction from which the cries seemed to come. But again, before much headway had been made, the noises stopped. Each time the boat stopped and the crew decided to return to land, the cries began. In the end, thoroughly confused, the crew turned finally and made for home. The cries had been heard quite distinctly by all the crew. A thorough investigation carried out later revealed no sign of any wreckage and the whole matter remained a mystery. About eight years after the incident, an Eriskay boat struck on a rock near Lingay and, though the crew members were saved, they were nearly drowned.

Instances of second sight are numerous, particularly in the Highlands where the ' gift ' is seemingly possessed by many people who prefer to keep their faculty in obscurity; and perhaps they are right to

do so for fear of causing unnecessary distress to
themselves and to their friends and neighbours. At
the turn of this century a woman lived on a farm
tucked away in the Rannoch hills. This woman was
known to have been descended from a long line of
women who had the 'gift.' One evening, after
market day at Aberfeldy, a farmer was making his
way home along the banks of the River Tay. In the
gathering darkness he slipped and fell into the
waters and was drowned. When he had not arrived
home the following morning, his wife called out
searchers to look for him, but they looked in vain.
The river was dragged and re-dragged for almost
three weeks and with nothing found but a hat and
stick. The missing man's family were by this time
in deep sorrow and were distressed by the thought
that the missing man was not to have a Christian
burial. But for that a body had to be found. The
family visited the woman at Rannoch, whom they
thought might be able to help them by her using
her gift. Now this woman had never seen Aberfeldy
and knew nothing of either the district or the
people. But she concentrated on her task and
eventually she reported that in some kind of a dream,
during which she claimed she was not asleep, she
saw a dead man in a reclining position, kept down
by some tree roots at the ' bottom of a bridge, at the
side of a river, below a queer bridge.'

The relatives of the missing man were at first
confused by the ' picture ' the woman had seen. It
was all too vague. However, the reference to the
' queer ' bridge gave them a clue. They sketched the

Aberfeldy Bridge and showed it to the woman, who recognised it at once.

'That is the bridge,' she said. 'And the hole below it is at the side.'

'But we have dragged that part in vain.'

'I can't help that,' she said, 'the body is there now.'

So a search party went off with a boat and grappling irons to the spot indicated and began a further search. In a short time the body of the missing and drowned man was recovered, just as the woman at Rannoch had 'seen' it.

There is another story which centres on the same area and the same woman. A shooting tenant of an estate in Rannoch took a lad of the district back with him to England to have him trained as a groom. Shortly afterwards news came back to Rannoch that this lad had disappeared and could not be found. The woman with the 'gift,' already mentioned, was appealed to for help. At first the appeal was thought to be hopeless, for she had never been to England in her life.

But she persevered and eventually 'saw,' first that the young lad had been murdered and buried among stones in a quarry near where he lived. This was not all, however. Scarcely had she seen all this than she 'saw' the murderers move the body from the quarry and fling it into a lake. The search for the lad commenced in England. Sure enough, a hole was found near the quarry and signs that many stones had been disturbed. Then the lake nearby was dragged and the Rannoch lad's body duly found.

At the beginning of the last war, the Committee for the Recording of Abnormal Happenings in Edinburgh received a letter from a woman who had had an unusual experience in August 1936 while she was at Culloden. She was wandering around the Highlanders' graves. 'Whether I was sufficiently steeped in atmosphere, I do not know; but certainly, when I lifted a square of Stuart tartan, which was blown down from the stone to the mound which is the grave, I distinctly saw the body of a very handsome dark-haired Highlander lying, as it were, at ease, on top of the mound.'

Realising that she was in fact seeing things and that the body was not a reality, except perhaps in the time of its own existence, two centuries previously, she fled from the spot.

Late in 1945 a man from Castle-Douglas was cycling home one night when he saw a light in front of him which he took to be a camp fire. As he approached the spot, he saw indeed a number of tinkers grouped round the fire with three or four horse-drawn caravans close by. He stopped and watched the scene for a moment, then made for home. It was not until afterwards that it crossed his mind that, though he had seen the encampment, he had heard no noise. The next morning, his mind full of curiosity, he cycled to the place where the camp should have been. But he found nothing: no tracks, no spent fire, no wheel marks, no marks of horses. What he had seen was a phantom tinkers' encampment.

. . . a furious storm blew up . . .

The story is still told and sung in the Western Isles of Allan Morrison and Annie Campbell. Allan was the son of a Stornoway merchant and was a noted sea captain. He generally traded with his ship between Stornoway and the Isle of Man. One morning in the spring of 1786 he left Stornoway to go to the island of Scalpay to see his betrothed, Annie, and to go through the ceremony of the marriage contract with her. But a furious storm blew up and Allan's ship was swamped. All the crew were lost and Annie Campbell grieved for her lost lover for many days until she herself died in utter despair.

Her body was placed in a coffin and taken on board a ship for burial at Rodel, at the southern tip of Harris. On the passage, that vessel, too, was over-taken by a violent storm during which the coffin was swept overboard into the raging seas. At the same moment as this occurred, it was claimed that a form was seen, supposed to be that of Allan, who bore it away into the depths of the sea. Shortly afterwards, Allan's body was found at the Shiant Isles in the Minch. And a few days later Annie's own body was found at exactly the same place. This event is well known in the Gaelic west, and the song *Ailean Duinn* has been known and sung for generations to commemorate the way in which the two lovers were eventually united in death.

Many years ago, in Skye, one of the annual Fairs was to be held in Portree. Shortly before the Fair was due, a young woman of the district of Kilmuir, about eighteen miles from Portree, was found in a state of depression, lamenting the catastrophe which she said would soon take place; a boat sinking in a storm in which many people drowned. At the time, people put this down to a dream or some other such occurrence and was duly forgotten. Later, on the evening of the market-day, a large boat left Portree for Kilmuir, crammed with people anxious to get home. But a storm rose up and all in the ship were consigned to a watery grave.

The following is an authenticated account of an experience in Kirriemuir, at the turn of this century:

'As I passed the house, what looked like a piece of diaphanous material appeared from the top of a *closed* window and disappeared rapidly upwards. I learned later that a newly-born child died in that room of the house at that time . . . '

One man claims that he owed his life to a ghost. He was living at the time in Forres, and his experience happened while he and a friend were looking for a farm which lay about ten miles east of Elgin.

It was an evening in late autumn and both men left about seven o'clock on their bicycles, without lamps. After they had travelled some miles along a country road, they found themselves quite lost. In any case, the darkness had fallen quicker than they had expected and they decided it was better to turn back. This they did, and as they came to the top of a steeply descending road one of the men said he would go forward alone and ask his friend to follow after a short interval, to avoid any collision or accident.

" I then went on alone, and was half-way down when a light suddenly appeared at the left-hand side of the road. I jumped off my bike and stared at this unexpected phenomenon. It was a thin column of light about six feet in height. While I stood there wondering, the light flickered for a few seconds and then vanished as mysteriously as it had appeared.

" A few minutes later I heard my friend approaching and shouted to him to dismount. When he did so, I explained my reason for stopping and standing there half-way down, when he would naturally have expected to find me at the foot of the hill. We then searched around for some time but found no natural explanation to account for this light. There were only green fields on both sides of the road and no animals, no dwellings within miles and no marshes where " marsh lights " might appear. After our fruitless search I suggested that we walk down the remainder of the steep road, and it was a lucky thing we did so. When we reached the bottom of the road we found a small stone bridge at right angles to the road. But for the warning light we must both have crashed over the bridge and sustained serious, if not fatal, injuries.'

The strange case of Sergeant Davies's ghost is recorded in the annals of Scottish legal history. The year was 1749, when, despite three years of military subjugation, the Highlands had not yet been pacified. The spirit of the clans was abroad, and though the hills might seem lonely at first glance, in fact they were alive with people hiding from the soldiers and skulking in caves, hollows and the wooded parts of the glens.

One evening in the summer of 1749, Sgt. Davies, of Guise's Regiment, marched from Aberdeen to Dubrach, in Braemar, with a party of eight privates. The business of the party was to conduct general surveillance in the district and particularly to obtain information of any disaffected persons who might be hiding in the district. The sergeant was a popular man, well-liked and newly married. His wife was to later bear witness to the fact that " he and she lived together in as great amity and love as any couple could do, and that he was never willing to stay away a night from her."

On the 28th September Sgt. Davies and his party met up with John Gowar in Glenclunie, who was wearing a tartan coat. This was, of course, at that time proscribed dress and Davies advised him not to use it in public. He then dismissed Gowar rather than take him prisoner. Shortly after this incident, Davies left his men to try for a shot at a stag he had spied. He was never seen again. His men searched for him in vain. Later, with a much enlarged search party, the hills in the area were scoured. But no trace of the missing sergeant was found.

In the following year, 1750, a shepherd, Alexander MacPherson, made it known that he was "greatly troubled by the ghost of Sergeant Davies, who had insisted that he should bury his bones."

MacPherson was instructed by the ghost to contact a Donald Farquharson, with whom Davies had lodged. MacPherson did so, and with Farquharson's help and acting on information given by the ghost, the sergeant's bones were eventually found in a peat moss. The ghost still appeared to MacPherson, however, and gave him to understand that two men were responsible for his death, one Duncan Clerk and one Alexander Bain MacDonald. Again, acting on the ghostly information, these two men were arrested in September 1753 and held in the Tollbooth, Edinburgh, on various charges, including that of the wearing of the kilt.

In the following year they were tried, and evidence was produced which proved that the men had indeed killed the sergeant. But the case for the defence was stronger and the two men were acquited. Thus, for all its trouble, the ghost of Sergeant Davies failed to get final satisfaction.

Another equally strange incident is firmly lodged

in legal history. This time it concerned the death of a pedlar, whose murderer was finally convicted on the evidence of a man who had dreamed of the place where the dead man's pack was lying and which was needed as material evidence in the case for the prosecution.

The pedlar's name was Murdock Grant and at the time of his death he was tramping round the district of Assynt, in Sutherland, selling his goods: silk handkerchiefs, prints, cottons and worsted stockings. The month was March and the year was 1830 when news came to the parish minister that the body of a pedlar had been found in a nearby loch. At first sight it seemed as if the pedlar had fallen in by accident, but investigation showed that the body had sustained wounds feloniously produced. Further investigation led to the arrest of one Hugh MacLeod, a native of Assynt, who was later taken to Inverness for his trial. He faced two charges. The first was the murder of the pedlar; the second was the theft of £30 in bank notes, a purse containing £6 in silver and the pedlar's pack.

The most damning evidence against MacLeod was his possession of a large amount of money which was unaccounted for. At the conclusion of the Crown's evidence with regard to this money came the most extraordinary testimony of the whole trial. This was given by one Kenneth Fraser, known as The Dreamer, who said that he had a number of times after the date of the pedlar's death been a drinking partner with MacLeod. He told the court of his dream, through which the pedlar's missing pack was found:

" I was at home when I had the dream in the month of February. It was said to me in my sleep by a voice, like a man's voice, that the pack was lying in sight of the place (where the murder took place). I got a sight of the place just as if I had been awake. I never saw the place before, but the voice said in Gaelic the pack of the merchant is lying in a cairn of stones in a hollow near to their house. When the officer came, I took him to the place I had got a sight of. It was on the south-west side of Loch Tor-na-eigin. We found nothing there, and we then went to search on the south side of the burn. I had not seen this place in my dream, but it was not far from the place I had seen in my dream that the things were found. There were five silk handkerchiefs."

This evidence, given by The Dreamer, concluded the case for the prosecution and, when the trial ended, a jury returned their verdict of guilty as libelled. On Monday, October 24, 1831, Hugh MacLeod was hanged in Inverness for the murder of the pedlar. Before a crowd of seven thousand or so onlookers, he confessed his guilt as he stood on the scaffold.

Late last century a minister went to visit a brother of his, a Captain MacLeod, who lived near Portree, Skye, and who had been ill for some time. After his visit he returned home, but the weather turned bad and he decided to lodge the night with a Mrs Nicolson at Scorriebreck. Her house was one of the larger houses on the island, with trap-stairs to the upper flats where all kinds of lumber were usually stored. In one corner of this attic was deposited the parish mort-cloth, kept there for safety and for convenience as the parish burial-place was nearby. Once her guest had been welcomed and settled in, Mrs Nicolson went up into the attic room to fetch some things and left her guest with her family in the parlour. They were startled to hear a loud scream, followed by the noise of a fall. They rushed to the upper floor with a light to find Mrs Nicolson in a fainting fit and quite insensible. She later recovered and told the minister that as she was in the attic she became aware of a brilliant light on the mort-cloth, which was spread over a table. In the middle of the light she saw the distinct image of his niece's face, the daughter of his brother, Captain MacLeod.

The story caused some concern at first, but was then forgotten — until shortly after when the young lady whose image had been seen took to her bed with an illness and died. Her bier was the first to require the use of the mort-cloth in question after that strange incident.

Another curious incident is also associated with Skye. This occurred in a miller's house in the northern part of the island. In the kitchen, and stacked round the open fire, were many planks of wood, recovered after a recent storm from the nearby shore. Wood, always scarce in the Hebrides, was a precious commodity and sea-sent material was more than welcomed.

On this particular evening the parish minister called on a visit. He was met by the miller's wife who told him that a neighbour, Christy MacLeod, a woman known as a seer, had been earlier sitting on a plank of wood in front of the fire when she suddenly fainted and fell to the floor. She was carried to a room at the other end of the house and laid on a bed until she recovered. The minister was asked to question the reason for the faint, which he did. Christy was quite recovered when he went into the room, and first avoided the direct questions put to her. Then she was persuaded to tell that

while she had been sitting on the wood she happened
to cast her eye on another plank nearby and saw
on it the stretched-out body, bleeding and mangled,
of a boy, MacDonald, who was at the time alive and
well. The minister then cautioned her to keep this
' sighting ' to herself.

Six weeks later the lad MacDonald was invited
to attend a wedding in another part of the parish,
to which he gladly went. On his return home, around
midnight and in extreme darkness, he lost his way
and fell over a precipice about a thousand feet high.
He was dashed to pieces in the clefts of rock and
debris below. When he was eventually missed, a
search party went out, involving almost the whole
of the parish. It was two days before the lad's body
was found, bruised and mangled, and held hard
and fast in a crevice. It was in such a bad condition
that it could not be carried easily, and the only
solution was to obtain a broad plank of wood. The
nearest dwelling with any wood to spare was the
miller's house.

There exists a vast literature on the subject of
dreams, and particularly their place in the foretelling of events to come. The following recorded
occurrence indicates perhaps an example of telepathy from the dying, rather than the dead, in that
the apparition experienced represents the deceased
as still existing. Taking the example further, which
is typical of many, but here given as a Scottish
instance, because it appears to contain a paranormal
element (e.g., an element of knowledge received
through no normal source), the dream may be taken

as evidence of the survival of the personality which manifested itself.

' Some 35 years ago I took into my employment a tender, delicate-looking boy, Robert MacKenzie, who, after some three or four years' service, suddenly left . . . A few years afterwards, my eye was caught by a youth of some 18 years of age ravenously devouring a piece of dry bread on the public street, and bearing all the appearance of being in a chronic state of starvation. Fancying I knew his features, I asked if his name was not MacKenzie. He at once became much excited, addressed me by name, and informed me that he had no employment; that his father and mother, who formerly supported him, were now both inmates of the ' poorhouse ' to which he himself had no claim for admission, being young and without any bodily disqualification for work, and that he was literally homeless and starving . . . Suffice it to say that he resumed his work, and that, under the circumstances, I did everything in my power to facilitate his progress . . . I was apparently his sole thought and consideration, saving the more common concerns of daily life.

' In 1862 I settled in London, and have never been in Glasgow since. Robert MacKenzie, and my workmen generally, gradually lost their individuality in my recollection. About 10 or 12 years ago my employees had their annual soiree and ball. This was always held . . . on a Friday evening . . . On the Tuesday morning following, immediately before 8 a.m., in my house on Campden Hill, I had the following manifestation, I cannot call it a dream;

but let me use the common phraseology. I dreamt, but with no vagueness as in common dreams, no blurring of outline or rapid passages from one thing disconnectedly to another, that I was seated at a desk, engaged in a business conversation with an unknown gentleman, who stood on my right hand.

'Towards me, in front, advanced Robert Mac-Kenzie, and, feeling annoyed, I addressed him with some asperity, asking if he did not see that I was engaged. He retired a short distance with exceeding reluctance, turned again to approach me, as if most desirous for an immediate colloquy, when I spoke to him still more sharply as to his want of manners. On this, the person with whom I was conversing took his leave, and MacKenzie once more came forward. "What is all this, Robert?" I asked, somewhat angrily. "Did you not see I was engaged?" "Yes, sir," he replied, "but I must speak with you at once." "What about?" I said, "what is it that can be so important?" "I wish to tell you, sir," he answered, "that I am accused of doing a thing I did not do, and that I want *you* to know it, and to tell you so, and that you are to forgive me for what I am blamed for, because I am innocent." Then, "I did not do the thing they say I did." I said, "What?" getting the same answer. I then naturally asked. "But how can I forgive you if you do not tell me what you are accused of?" I can never forget the emphatic manner of his answer, in the Scottish dialect, "Ye'll sune ken." This question and the answer were repeated at least twice — I am certain the answer was repeated thrice, in the most fervid tone.

' On that I awoke, and was in that state of surprise and bewilderment which such a remarkable dream might induce, and was wondering what it all meant, when my wife burst into my bedroom, much excited, and holding an open letter in her hand, exclaimed, " Oh, James, here's a terrible end to the workmen's ball, Robert MacKenzie has committed suicide! " With now a full conviction of the meaning of the vision, I at once quietly and firmly said, " No, he has not committed suicide." " How can you possibly know that? " " Because he has just been here to tell me."

' I have purposely not mentioned in its proper place, so as not to break the narrative, that on looking at MacKenzie I was struck by the peculiar appearance of his countenance. It was of an indescribable bluish-pale colour, and on his forehead appeared spots which seemed like blots of sweat. For this I could not account, but by the following post my manager informed me that he was wrong in writing of suicide. That, on Saturday night, MacKenzie, on going home, had lifted a small black bottle containing *aqua fortis* (which he used for staining the wood on birdcages, made for amusement), believing this to be whisky, and pouring out a wineglassful, had drunk it off at a gulp, dying on the Sunday in great agony. Here, then, was the solution of his being innocent of what he was accused of — suicide, seeing that he had inadvertently drunk *aqua fortis*, a deadly poison . . .

'My manager first heard of the death on the Monday — wrote me on that day as above — and on the Tuesday wrote again explaining the true facts. The dream was on the Tuesday morning, immediately before the 8 a.m. post delivery, hence the thrice emphatic "Ye'll sune ken." I attribute the whole to MacKenzie's yearning gratitude for being rescued from a deplorable state of starvation, and his earnest desire to stand well in my opinion. I have coloured nothing, and leave my readers to draw their own conclusions.'

6

TALES OF HORROR

WHILST many ghosts tend to operate in their own time in the past, and almost ignore the living person who observes them, there are some which seem able to project themselves into another time, the present, and exhibit signs of malevolence towards those whom they meet. Whether the malevolence is intentional or not, there are many who have recorded their experiences which almost put fictional ghost stories to shame for their false inventions. The following stories have been collected from many sources over various parts of Scotland and serve to indicate the rather terrifying experiences of those persons who had the misfortune to come into contact, often unintentionally, with the spirits of the long-dead.

There are a number of haunted houses in Glasgow. Most of these were buildings in which have occurred such deeds as murders and suicides. Here, in fact, may lie the reason for the seeming malevolence of some ghosts which seek some kind of vengeance on the present living for the sufferings they had to endure at the hands of another living person in their own time-scale.

19th century Glasgow

One particular house in the neighbourhood of Blythswood Square in Glasgow was many years ago the subject of interest from a prospective buyer. He was taken with the whole building — except for the bathroom. This room struck him as being excessively grim; its atmosphere and general appearance upset him, though for what reason he could not say. It was a room, he recorded later, that he would prefer to remain outside when in the house by himself. In the event, his wife being so taken with the house, it was purchased, but not before the bathroom had been thoroughly modernised and painted, with a new, gleaming white bath surrounded by wood.

But even with this alteration, the owner felt decidedly uncomfortable whenever he was in the bathroom; this although other members of his family felt nothing at all. The owner compromised by leaving the door ajar while he attended to his shaving and bathing; but his wife insisted that the door should always be shut, and that was that.

One night he decided he must put his fears to the test. So he went along with a lighted candle to have a hot bath — with the door of the room firmly locked from the inside.

Though quite uneasy for no apparent reason at all, he ran hot water from a gas geyser and undressed. As he was testing the heat of the water, a sound in the unlit firegrate made him turn round. But he saw nothing. Thinking it might have been something dropping from the chimney above, he turned his attention once more to his bath. Again, that noise from the grate. But, once more, nothing to indicate the source. After investigating the grate thoroughly, he turned to make for the bath when he slipped and fell on the floor. For some seconds he lay still, recovering his senses and then made to raise himself. Suddenly his candle went out and he found himself in funereal blackness. Quite startled by now, he sensed a rising feeling of terror and his first thought was to get to the door of the bathroom to cry out for more matches for his candle.

Then, quite without warning, there came from the bath the sounds of rubbing and splashing, as though some person was washing vigorously. The water rose and fell, bubbled and gurgled. As if to add to the realism of the sounds, there came gasping and puffing and the soft, smooth sound of a well-soaped flannel.

The next thing to occur was the opening of a cupboard door, slowly and stealthily, and the owner, transfixed in his terror, heard something approach in his direction. Whatever it was came up to him and something touched his naked skin. This was the hemline of silk petticoats, from which exuded the perfume of violets. His terror increased when the ghost of the woman, for such it was, stepped on his chest, placing an icy-cold, high-heeled shoe on him as though he were a doormat. But the ghost was oblivious of his presence. Next, there came the sound of a movement as though the woman had reached the bath, to be followed by violent splashing and gasping. The noises of the bather grew weaker and finally ceased, when the woman turned from the murder which she had obviously committed and made for the fireplace.

The deep blackness in the room was now broken by the sight of the white, luminous face of a woman who was obviously beautiful but whose beauty had turned into something repellent with hate.

Then the face vanished and the owner eventually made for the door of the room, unlocked it, and managed to reach the safety of his bedroom. As with the other times when he had confessed to his wife his uneasiness about the room, she scoffed at his fears and told him to think no more of the matter.

For some days nothing more untoward occurred until one morning when the eldest son in the family was running a bath, he saw, floating in the bath, the body of an old, grey-haired man. It was bloated and had a purple hue; glassy eyes stared at the ceiling. The boy screamed and ran from the room. The household immediately went to the bathroom to investigate the matter, but found nothing in the bath.

The father had remained in the dining room; his own terrifying experience had been sufficient for him. Chiding the boy for his imagination, the family went out into the landing, to come face to face with a handsome woman dressed in costly silks and jewellery. She glided past them with silent footsteps and disappeared into a cupboard.

The reason for the owner's uneasiness was now confirmed. Within a week the house was empty and up for sale. Later inquiries revealed that at one time the house had belonged to a rich old man who had married a beautiful young woman of Spanish descent. The disparity in ages led to quarrels. The man was eventually found dead in his bath; there being no indications of violence, it was generally supposed that he had fainted and accidentally drowned. The young widow, who had inherited all the money, left the house, went abroad and was never seen again.

Still in Glasgow, another house gave the occupant of one of its rooms more than some cause for concern. When the following events occurred, it had been converted into a first-class private hotel, innocent on the outside but containing the essence of something which awaited only the right kind of recipient. The latter eventually turned up, an actor who was playing in Glasgow. For the first three nights in this particular room nothing happened — except that the actor had the most terrifying nightmares, which was unusual for him.

On the fourth night he was awakened by the sound of a loud crash. He sat up and listened for a time, but heard nothing more. Thinking that he had heard the sound in his sleep, he decided that a drink of lime juice from a bottle he kept on the mantelpiece would help to cool his rushing brain. He got up and, in the darkness, made his way to the mantelpiece, first to find matches and then the juice. But try as he might, he could not find the place. Deciding to give up the drink, he groped his way back to the bed, guiding himself by feel round the items of furniture in the room with which he had become familiar. But then he found he could not trace the bed. It was a room of reasonably small dimensions and it seemed to him at first almost a joke that he could lose a bed in such a room. He tried again, but failed. Then, as he stretched his arms in front of him, his fingers came into contact with a noose suspended in mid-air.

Almost as if in a dream, he felt his feet glued to the floor and the noose, with a strange and gentle purring sound, fall about his neck and begin to tighten.

In a mounting feeling of desperation he tried to raise his hands to remove the rope, but found that some power forced them down to his side again. He opened his mouth to cry out, but was unable to utter any sound. Only a cold, icy current of air froze in his lungs. He felt cold, clammy hands tearing his feet from the floor. He was hoisted up and then dropped. A sharp pain shot through his body. He made frantic efforts to release himself, but could not. Then he blacked out. When he recovered he found himself lying on the floor of the room, apparently suffering from nothing else but a chill.

The next night, determined to prevent a recurrence of what he had experienced, he left a candle burning and went to sleep. Later in the night he woke up in darkness. A curious smell attracted his notice. At first he thought he was dreaming, but the smell grew stronger, the pungent odour of drugs or, at the very least, the same strong smell as one meets in an old chemist's shop. As his mind tried to grasp what was happening to him, his face came in contact with something cold and flabby. This caused him to react so violently that he fell out of bed and onto the floor.

The fall convinced him of one thing — that he was not dreaming. Getting up to go into bed again, he froze in his movements. For he saw the bed was occupied. In the middle of the pillow was a face: the face of his brother who at the time was supposed to be living in New York. His brother's appearance was startling: the mouth was open, the tongue was swollen, and the face was a yellow colour tinged with a livid, lurid black. Then the brother spoke: 'I have been wanting to speak to you for ages, but something I cannot explain has always prevented me. I have been dead a month; not cancer, but Dolly. Poison. Good-bye. I shall rest in peace now.'

The voice stopped. There was a rush of cold air, faintly scented with the odour of drugs, and then the face vanished.

The following morning a letter arrived from Dolly, his brother's wife, to say that the brother had died of cancer in the throat.

The experience of a couple who were touring Scotland in the years of the 1880s is particularly interesting in that the spirit manifestation caused terror and physical sickness. The couple arrived in Dundee and were directed to a hotel, previously an inn, near the Perth Road. They were delighted with the place at first sight. Being an old building, it exuded a pleasant atmosphere of old-world charm. The interior was no less pleasing: low ceilings, oak beams, polished wood floors, diamond-lattice windows and numerous nooks and crannies. The hotel was full, however, and the only accommodation the proprietor could offer was a room at the end of a long passage leading to the back of the building. It was a large room, with a big ebony four-poster bed in a recess. A deep and dark cupboard was let into the wall directly facing the bed.

The couple were not at all superstitious, except in so far as they discussed how many memories were associated with such an old building. More than that was not discussed. Yet, when the couple undressed for bed the woman sensed a curious sensation as she rummaged in the cupboard.

Some time after, a nearby church tower bell had struck midnight, the woman woke to become aware of a smell in the room. It was pungent and most offensive. It was so strong that it crept up her nostrils and brought her out in a cold release of perspiration. The smell overpowered her and she decided to trace it, half-knowing in her mind that it could not be other than associated with something horrible and strange. She got up from the bed, taking care not to wake her husband, and traced the source of the smell to the same dark cupboard which had upset her earlier. By the time she reached the cupboard door the stench was almost suffocating. She paused for a few minutes; one voice within her told her to get back to her bed, but the other told her to satisfy her curiosity and open the door.

At last, the latter voice dominated and she opened the door. No sooner had she done so than the room began to fill with a faint phosphorescent glow and she saw opposite her a human head floating in mid-air. It was the head of a man, red-haired and in an advanced state of decay. She was petrified and quite unable to cry out to her husband. Then, as the head began to move towards her, she screamed and fled to the bed, followed by the floating head. Her husband woke up at the sound and was even more terrified than his wife as the head hovered over the bed. He tried to utter a prayer, but not one syllable came from his dry throat.

He managed to stretch out his hand to the floor of the room and grasp his walking stick. With both hands, he brought it down on the head. The result was as they might have expected. The stick met with no resistance and came down on the bedclothes. The head continued its advance towards them. The couple jostled to get out of the bed together, and in their haste both fell on the floor. With the head now hovering over them, they could do nothing but watch it in terror. It descended lower and lower until it passed right through them and through the floor; then it vanished.

The couple took the next few hours until dawn to recover from their experience, and in the morning demanded an explanation from the landlord. At first he was reluctant to offer any explanation, and tried to convince them that it had been a nightmare. But they insisted and were eventually told the story.

' What am I to do? I cannot shut up a house on which I have taken a twenty years' lease, and, after all, there is only one visitor in twenty who is disturbed by the apparition. What is the history of the head? It is said to be that of a pedlar who was murdered here over a hundred years ago. The body was hidden behind the wainscoting, and his head hidden under the cupboard floor. The miscreants were never caught; they are supposed to have gone down in a ship that sailed from this port just about that time and was never heard of again.'

A hotel, now demolished, in Aberdeen was the scene of another mysterious manifestation. On this particular occasion a nurse was called in to look after one of the hotel guests, a Miss Vining. The hotel proprietor knew nothing about his guest except that she had been an actress and was now ill of a disease which was oriental in origin. The nurse was required to be with her patient almost continuously. Her first meeting with Miss Vining was strange. No sooner had she entered the sick room than she became aware of a gloom which seemed to hang over her like a huge shadow. And when she approached the sick woman on her bed, the feeling she received was of something trying to force itself between her and her patient.

The patient being too ill even to converse, the nurse settled down beside the bed for a vigil. Contrary to her expectations, the first night passed without incident. On the second night, however, at about ten o'clock, she had just registered her patient's temperature and had sat down when something caused her to look across to a chair on the other side of the bed. It was occupied by a child, a tiny girl.

Rather startled at the sight, she rose to chide the child for being in the sickroom, and to ask how she entered the room without being noticed. But the child lifted a hand and motioned her back. Unable to help herself, the nurse stood where she was. How long she was almost entranced she did not know. Then, a long-drawn-out sigh from her patient took her attention. Again she made to move but was once more stilled by the raised hand of the child. She sat down, and then, so overcome by her efforts to remove the state of inertia into which the child had placed her, she fell asleep. When she later woke there was no sign of the child. She turned her attention to the patient who was delirious and had a high temperature. Administering her drugs, the temperature was reduced and Miss Vining relaxed until the hours of the morning.

Telling the doctor of the child's visit, the nurse was told that on no account was any person to visit the sick woman and advised her to lock the door of the bedroom. The next night, with the door firmly locked, the nurse settled down to a night's vigil. The long hours passed and she nodded off. A sob from her patient roused her and, looking at the bed, caught sight of the same child again. Once more the nurse rose to chase the child away when, raising her small hand, the child's power virtually paralysed the nurse.

A long time passed as the child sat there watching the sick woman endure another delirious spell, and the nurse sat transfixed, unable to do or say anything. Then, at last, the child rose and moved from the bed towards the window. The nurse found her voice and cried after the child. She reached over and snatched the child's hat. It melted away in her hand and, to her horror, the child's face, previously pretty, now turned into the face of a corpse of a Hindu child with a big, gaping cut in its throat. At that sight the nurse fainted.

When she recovered, all ghostly manifestations were gone. And the patient was dead. One of her hands was thrown across her eyes, as if to shut out some object on which she feared to look, while the other hand grasped the counterpane with a grip of terror.

After the burial, the nurse was asked by the hotel proprietor to pack up Miss Vining's things, among which was found a photograph of a Hindu child dressed in the same clothes as was worn by the ghostly child. On the reverse of the picture were the words: ' Natalie. May God forgive us both.'

Nothing more was ever seen of the child ghost or of the Hindu child. But not long after Miss Vining's death, the hotel became haunted — by the ghost of a woman.

A most unusual story is associated with a house near Ayr. It was a two-storey building, with a main wing and a side construction. It was full of rooms and wandering corridors, leading from the large hall which sported a gallery running round it. This house was haunted by a golden light which had the perfume of heliotropes. On one occasion a visitor to the house, so charmed with the whole building and its casual planning, decided to explore. After spending some time in the main building, a search was begun on the side construction. At the foot of its ivy-covered walls and straight in their centre was a wide bed of white flowers; no flowers of other colours were seen. Though curious at the sight of the garden, the visitor thought it best not to enquire as to the reason for the lack of colour. Some evenings later the visitor made a careful way in the dark towards that side of the house next to the new wing. Arriving at the end of a long corridor, she found herself in the middle of the gallery overlooking the large entrance hall. Making further progress, she was stopped by a cry from near at hand. It was a blood-curdling shriek which began in a low key and climbed up through the spine and into the mind to end in a high-pitched piercing. In a sweat of fear she looked around but saw nothing and the house was silent.

After a few moments she proceeded down the next corridor and eventually came to the side wing. Glancing through the window, to where the garden of white flowers lay, she caught sight of, not white flowers, but golden blooms. Then, as she looked, the garden disappeared and its place was taken by a room. Again, as she took in all the details of the furniture, the large open bay window, and the decoration, a door opened and in walked a young girl, carrying a bunch of heliotrope. Less than a moment later, the girl stepped back. A wild wave of terror distorted her face and the room disappeared to leave the scene a simple garden of white flowers.

The next morning, the visitor mentioned what she had seen and was told of the occasion when, forty years previously, the garden had in fact been a room extension, since taken down and replaced by the garden. One night, the house was broken into by burglars, through the window of the room. A relation of the owners was sleeping in it at the time, and with the noise of the intruders she woke and screamed. In panic and in a fit of desperation, the burglars murdered the girl to silence her. Her haunting, since the tragedy, has since been in the form of a shaft of light followed by a scent of heliotrope.

Glamis Castle has been mentioned elsewhere with regard to its ghostly associations. The castle is of an ancient though uncertain date; it is reckoned to have been in existence at the beginning of the eleventh century. From time to time, extra building has changed the original shape, and interior alterations have taken place, but the traditional associations with the supernatural have hardly changed at all. It is said that in the castle tower

Glamis Castle

there is a room, hidden in some unexpected quarter, which is known only to three people at any one time. The following story is the experience of a woman who stayed at Glamis Castle late last century.

At her own request, placing no credence in the stories she had heard about the hauntings, she was given a bedroom in the tower. On her first night, before she retired, she had a good supper and then climbed into bed. Within minutes she was asleep. Then she woke up — and found herself in an oddly-shaped room with a high ceiling. The floor was of blackened oak. A window was set high up in the wall, quite inaccessible from the floor. The walls were covered with some kind of drapery. The furniture seemed to her to be more appropriate to the cell of a prison or lunatic asylum. There was no chair; only a coarse deal table, a straw mattress and a kind of trough. An air of irrepressible gloom hung about the place, which increased in its intensity as she looked with mounting fear.

For some inexplicable reason she found herself, not in her bed, but standing in the room with her eyes fixed on one corner. It was in the shadow and nothing with any kind of shape was discernible. Then something moved. The gentle rubbing of a soft body on the floor, breathing, one or two small cracking noises and slowly the thing in the corner began to make itself known. The body was hunched. The legs were crooked and mis-shapen. The arms were unduly long, with crooked, knotty fingers. The head was large and bestial, with hair that fell around the face in tangled masses. In a slow, lumbering movement, the shape lunged towards the onlooker. Before anything else could happen, the handle of the door turned and another person entered; at the same time, the whole tower seemed to reverberate with the most appalling animal screams. Then she found herself sitting up in bed with the screams still in her ears only, for the night and her room were as silent as they had always been.

Another woman had an experience which remained with her for the rest of her life. She, too, was given a room in the tower of Glamis Castle and was a firm sceptic whenever the subject of ghosts cropped up.

On her first night, after a long journey from Edinburgh, she was glad of the comfort of her bed, and fell asleep the moment her head touched the pillow. But not for long. Even through her deep sleep she was startled awake by the sound of a loud noise. She listened for it again, but all was silent. Then, as the minutes fled by, she became aware of an unnatural feeling in the air, as though the silence was a prelude to some coming event. As she listened further, she heard a low, distinct noise, repeated in rapid succession. She realised that the sound was that of mailed footsteps racing up the long flight of stairs at the end of the corridor leading to her room. The sounds drew nearer and grew louder. Almost outside the door of her room there came other noises: the banging and clanking of sword scabbards, the panting and gasping of men, sore pressed and obviously fighting for their lives. Two men in particular were fighting a duel to the death. Through the stout wood of the door, the listener heard every detailed noise made by the men, including, once, when one of the men was hurled back by a tremendous blow which sent him reeling heavily against the door. The blow was repeated and a cry rose in the victim's throat that developed into a gurgling groan.

Immediately there followed the distinct sound of

a body drained of life slithering in heavy armour down against the door; then followed the final clang of metal as the victim fell dead. There was a pause, as though the victor was considering his next move. A movement under the door attracted her attention. Slowly, taking its time, a dark stream of fluid lapped its way into the room. In her dismay the woman screamed aloud. There was a sudden stir from outside the room, and the next moment — despite the fact that the door was securely locked — it slowly opened. The limits of her endurance reached saturation point at that moment and she fainted, to wake up some hours later with a welcome stream of morning sunshine coming in from her window.

With some doubt, she argued that her experience had been the result of extreme exhaustion after the journey from Edinburgh, and chose to sleep in the same room on the following night. After a day spent walking on the moors, she lay down on her bed and dozed off in a light sleep. Suddenly she woke up to find herself face to face with a huge figure in bright armour. The visor was up, and from the opening a face leered at her; a face long since dead, but still with the smile of the living on it. The figure bent lower over her, and before anything further could happen a rap on the door, heralding a maid with some tea, caused the figure to vanish.

A final story about the castle reads more like fiction, but is related as being true in its details. About the middle of last century a man was lodging at a hotel near the Strathmore Estate. Having a deep interest in antiquities, he went into the castle grounds one day. Looking around, he was met by a man whom he took to be a gardener. The man's features were unusual: high cheek-bones, a mass of red hair, and a hawk-like shape to the face. He asked the gardener if he knew of any antique objects found in the grounds of the castle. The latter said that he had something of particular interest, and both men went down a track to a cottage.

The item was in fact the skeleton of a hand, with abnormally large knuckles, and the first joint — of both fingers and thumb — much shorter than the others.

The item was indeed unusual, so much so that the gardener was offered a good price for the relic. But the gardener refused the money, and offered it free, with words of caution that it was not a canny thing to have about one's house.

The caution went unheeded, for the buyer was a hard-headed man from London who paid no attention to the superstitions of Highlanders, who saw fairies as often as they blinked their eyes.

That evening, he studied the skeleton hand by candlelight. It was indeed an unusual specimen for his collection, and he warmed in anticipation of the envious comments his friends would make. Towards midnight he decided to retire and was about to put his things away when he caught sight of the mirror opposite him. In it he saw the door of his room was open. He turned round to close the door, but saw it was already closed. Thinking he had experienced an optical illusion, he looked in the mirror again :

the door was open. Then, as he looked into the mirror more closely he fancied he saw a large black shadow in the doorway. A shiver ran up his spine and for a moment he felt a pang of fear. He turned round — the door was as firmly shut as it had been the last time he looked.

Despite some misgivings, he decided to keep looking in the mirror to see what was about to happen. The darkness in the doorway was there when he looked again, only this time it moved to take the shape of a huge spider or some odd-shaped bird. But the whole was so indistinct that he was unable to say exactly what it was. Slowly the shadow drew near to him and the experience so fascinated him that even if he had been able to, he felt he must remain seated to participate in what he felt sure was about to happen. The next thing he realised was that the shadowy form coming closer to him was forming into a hand — the skeleton of the hand he had got from the gardener at Glamis Castle. This time, however, the hand was covered with mouldering flesh. It moved towards the back of his chair and then he felt its cold and clammy touch on his head. It pressed downwards and almost suffocated him. Yet, all this was happening to him as he looked in the mirror. It was as though his imagination had run riot.

Suddenly he found himself in a room from which all his familiar furniture had disappeared. It was bare and comfortless, strangely constructed, without a door. Only a narrow slit of a window near the ceiling admitted light.

In one corner of the room lay a mattress on which lay a form, huddled up as though in the cold. He found, to his surprise, that he had a knife in his hands and, try as he did, he could not dispel the thoughts of murder that were forming in his mind. With a cold and calculating stealth, he approached the mattress. With his hand raised high, he brought the knife down and plunged it into the side of the form. Then he recrossed the room and found himself in his hotel apartment once more.

His first reaction was to look for the skeleton of the hand. But it was not where he had left it. It had vanished completely. His room door was still shut. A final reaction was to look in the mirror and he saw, not his own face, but that of the gardener leering out of the glass.

The following day, intent on getting some further explanation about the skeleton hand, he went to Glamis Castle and looked for the gardener. Unable to find him, he decided to call in at the cottage, but was unable to find the building. Enquiries revealed that no one knew about the cottage, nor did they know of the gardener. Completely mystified, he returned to London by way of Edinburgh.

Stopping in the capital for a day or so, he took it in his mind to visit a loan exhibition of pictures in one of the city's galleries. As he wandered past the portraits, all thoughts of his terrifying experience gone from his mind, he halted abruptly. Before him was the portrait of a gentleman in an ancient costume, with the face of the gardener of Glamis Castle. The thick red hair, the hawk-like features and leering eyes were those of the character he had met in the grounds of the castle, but who did not exist except, perhaps, in his own time in the past.

7

HAUNTED HOUSES

HAUNTED houses abound throughout the Scottish countryside. The house is probably more often associated with ghostly manifestations than more obvious places such as churchyards. Ghosts in no way seem to confine themselves to old buildings, as might again be expected. Comparatively recent dwellings such as Council houses have their fair share of ghostly happenings, unexplained noises and unnerving sights. In more than a few instances of ghostly manifestations in occupied houses the residents have resorted to exorcism to get rid of their unwanted and uninvited guests. Other people accept the supernatural and allow their ghost to wander around. But it all really depends on the ghost (poltergeists are particularly troublesome and tend to make life difficult), and many houses have had to be abandoned to their spirit occupants, attempts at excorcism having been completely futile.

Before Andrew Carnegie, the multi-millionaire, bought Skibo Castle, in Sutherland, the place was said to be haunted. The story relates that the castle was on one occasion left in the sole charge of a man-servant who had a particularly evil turn of mind. One night he induced his sweetheart, a local girl whom he had betrayed, to visit him at the castle. This the girl agreed to do. But when she failed to return from her visit, a hue and cry was raised. Despite an intensive search, she was never found. In time suspicion fell on the castle servant. The whole building was subjected to a thorough search. The fellow protested his innocence; the missing girl was not found, and the whole affair became a local mystery. Shortly afterwards the servant left both the castle and the district and, soon after he had done so, people living in the castle found themselves to be regularly startled by unearthly screams in the corridors and by the sight of the ghost of a young woman who appeared always to be in great terror. Many years passed until some repairs were required in the castle buildings, during which a woman's bones were found in the very spot at which the apparition usually disappeared. The remains were buried elsewhere, since when the castle ceased to be haunted.

Another house in Sutherland had to be abandoned because of a weird vision which regularly appeared before the tenants and terrified them so greatly that they had to flee for their sanity. One local ex-soldier, brave and fearless in the field of battle and as brave before the unknown, offered to spend a night in the house. This he did, and when the ghost eventually appeared he, despite heartbeats thudding against his chest, asked it the reason for its visits. It replied that its body had been buried beneath the floor of

the house and if it were to be decently interred in
the churchyard it would cease to haunt the house.
The following day a search was made and the bones
were duly found, buried in the churchyard as
requested, and the house became habitable again.

One house in Ross-shire was haunted by a series
of inexplicable noises and voices. These a local man
decided to investigate and undertook to sleep in
the place alone. Shortly before midnight he was
awakened by the sound of rats scurrying about in an
adjoining room. He thumped a chair beside his
bed and the noises stopped. Less than an hour later
he was again wakened, this time by a sound as if a
hard broom were sweeping the floor in the next room
in a very noisy fashion. This time he decided he
would investigate and rose to light his lamp. Before
he could strike a match he heard a voice in Gaelic
plead: ' Let me in, let me in.'

He struck his match, and as soon as he had done
so the voice stopped. He listened carefully for some
time, but all was silent in the house. He fell asleep
again, and for a third time his slumber was disturbed
by the rattling of the bedroom door and a feeble
voice saying: ' I cannot harm you, but leave this
place soon, do, do.'

There was such a degree of substance and reality
in the voice that he decided the best course of action
was to get a neighbour along to help him search the
place, being now convinced that a human agency
was behind his experiences. So he dressed and went
along to the next house. But the neighbour refused
to go along with him. However, he did compensate

his unwillingness by telling the story of the house which had been built on the site of an older thatched dwelling from which a poor widow had been forcibly evicted. Before she left she had cursed the new house and all who would ever live in it. While the new house was being built, mysterious lights were often seen flickering about in the uncompleted building. Workmen's tools were found scattered about on several occasions; one of the tenants had become bankrupt and died after a short illness; and another tenant had committed suicide. Eventually the tenants had to leave the place, so unnerved did they become at the ghostly manifestations. Later, as it was a good-built house, other tenants took over and that family were quite happy in it and were never at any time disturbed by any inexplicable and hair-raising noises.

One rather malevolent ghost is that of ' Terrible William,' otherwise Lord Soulis, who is said to haunt Hermitage Castle in Roxburghshire. He had the reputation of being a skilful practitioner of the black arts. Local tradition has it that to get the best out of his magical rites, he would kidnap local children, imprison them in the castle's dungeons, and keep them until he was ready to use them in his foul rites, murdering them and using their blood to make his magic more effective. When eventually news of his deeds became known, the people of the nearby village stormed the building, took him prisoner, bound him in chains, and threw him into a cauldron of boiling lead. After this execution of rough justice, his ghost was seen in and around the castle reenacting the deeds of his erstwhile bad life. In his lifetime he was supposed to have made a pact with Satan who appeared in front of him wearing a cap stained red with the blood of his victims. In exchange for his soul, Lord Soulis was rewarded with the right to summon the Devil by rapping three times on an iron chest.

Fyvie Castle

Fyvie Castle, in Aberdeenshire, has a ghost room, a murder room, and a secret room. The famous ' Green Lady ' ghost was seen in 1920 wandering about the castle's corridors and disappearing through the panels of a dark wainscotted apartment. A few years before, when a great ugly mass of fungus had appeared in the gun-room, workers discovered a complete skeleton. It was after these bones were removed that disturbances were experienced in the castle. They ceased only when the owner, Lord Beith, requested that the skeleton be rebuilt into the wall again.

Crathes Castle also has its haunted room. A woman, yet another ' Green Lady,' is frequently seen to cross the room and make for an unusually fine carved timber fireplace. When she reaches this spot she is seen to lift a ghostly baby from the hearth. A number of years ago, when workmen were effecting repairs and alterations in the building, the bones of a woman and child were found beneath this fireplace.

Leith Hall, near Kennethmont, Aberdeenshire, is an old family house with a charm of its own. The original nucleus was built about 1650: a rectangular tower house with twin turrets at each of the gables, erected by James Leith. The vicissitudes of the Leith and the Leith-Hay families have filled the house and its grounds with romantic features. The name Hay was added to that of Leith in 1789, on the death of Andrew Hay of Rannes, a Jacobite and pardoned ' rebel ' whose lands were inherited by the Leiths. In the grounds is the Dule Tree, from which malefactors were hanged in the days of heritable jurisdiction. The house, perhaps inevitably, has some interesting ghost associations.

Elizabeth Byrd, the author, has recounted many of her experiences while living in Leith Hall in her book, *A Strange and Seeing Time*. Ghostly noises

Leith Hall

have been heard (a pibroch of pipe music with counterpoint of drums, and a chanted Mass); ghost smells have been experienced: of food and camphor; sounds, such as heavy footsteps on the third floor and doors closing; and, of course, visual images. The ghost of a woman has been seen in the Historic Wing of the house. Loud, angry voices have been heard on occasions. Miss Byrd's husband, Barrie Gaunt, has related his experience in the haunted master bedroom. He had gone to bed early, but woke about midnight to have a glass of water and enjoy a cigarette. About five minutes after he had put out the light and turned over to go to sleep, he felt — *knew,* he confesses — that someone was

moving towards him through the darkness. He
relates that he was literally paralysed with horror;
for the thing that came towards him was malignant.
" Ghosts are not supposed to attack one physically,
but I felt that such an attack was imminent." Mr
Gaunt found that, try as he might, he could not
move. " It was a sort of muscular paralysis. Nor
could I seem to catch my breath. I've never felt that
sort of fear before . . . About two terrible minutes
went by. Then, with my eyes closed so as not to see
it, I was able to lunge cross the bed, fumble for the
light and turn it on. There was nothing visible."

This kind of experience is common to those who
for some reason are unable to ' see ' visual images,
but are only too aware of their ability to sense some
kind of presence, particularly when it has a malignant character. The writer has had this kind of
unpleasant experience and can vouch for the sense
of terror it brings and the almost superhuman effort
that is required not to succumb to an overwhelming
desire to ' go under ' in a swoon of complete and
dark oblivion, which may well be the intention of
the visiting spirit.

Elizabeth Byrd has recorded that she spent two
years alone in that same bedroom, but only towards
the end of that period did she sense a feeling of
uneasiness before she saw the ghost.

Alanna Knight, the Aberdeen author, has also
had paranormal experiences in Leith Hall, and
particularly in the nursery where she had a series
of " waking dreams " in which she identified with
a child accompanied by a governess.

One last, but by no means least, anecdote about Leith Hall, this time from Donella Gordon, of Elgin, who once worked at the hall, in 1929: "The Hon. Lady allowed us to have in our boy friends one night a week. I will never forget, a young couple went along for a quiet spell to the Gun Room, that is under the Music Room. The rest of us were preparing to have our tea and the cakes when along came this young couple. His face was deathly white and his hair standing on end. The girl was sick with fear. They said someone had walked from the Music Room to the Leith bedroom above them *in chains,* moaning and groaning. I know that when we maids had duties in the Leith bedroom we always felt that someone or something would step out of the shadows." It was in this bedroom that Mr Gaunt saw the ghost of a Victorian ' nanny ' in broad daylight, surrounded by tourist sightseers.

About three miles from Dingwall, Easter Ross, stands the house of Mountgerald, said to be haunted by the ghost of a workman who was killed during its construction and buried beneath the foundations as a sacrifice. His ghost has been seen on a number of occasions around the spot where he was killed (a large block of stone fell on him) in a large cellar at the bottom of the stairs leading to the basement. To this spot the ghost of the unfortunate man is bound for all time except for five nights in each year: at New Year, Midsummer, the Spring and Autumn Solstices, and on the anniversary of his death, which occurs in the middle of the month of August. As he had been in life a disliked and vindictive kind of person, so he is in death, and he is said to be capable of wreaking his vengeance on anyone sleeping in the house on his ' free ' nights. One friend of previous tenants of Montgerald died on the evening of the August anniversary, who had otherwise been in good health.

The Doune of Rothiemurchus, Inverness-shire, has a ghost and a haunted room, according to local tradition and ken.

A curious story was once in common circulation in the Isle of Harris, Outer Hebrides. This concerned the ' Coffee House ' at Leverburgh. Many years ago, about the 1850s, a building was erected by the Countess of Dunmore, the proprietrix of Harris, for the purpose of providing fishermen with a place for meals, and to offer some suitable accommodation to casual travellers in the islands. For many years, the house proved to be a popular meeting place, both for local people and visitors on both business and pleasure. The story of the Coffee House has its origins just after the turn of this century when many strange knocking sounds began to be heard and cause no end of disturbance to the occupants. The noises, it was noticed, were particularly confined to an area in the region of a bedroom which was occupied by some maids working in the house. The knocking noises often became so unbearable that there was talk of abandoning the building; indeed, the point was eventually reached where the occupants became afraid to sleep in the house alone.

Several weeks after these noises began, the maids

were transferred to a room in another part of the house. But the knocking followed them to their new room. Just when the owners became desperate with despair, one of the maids approached the mistress of the house and said that she was leaving her employ. Thinking that the reason for the girl's sudden decision was the noises, the girl said: 'The knocking has nothing to do with you. It follows me wherever I go.' And, indeed, the knocking stopped on the day this maid left Leverburgh. Afterwards there were no further disturbances experienced in the house. A couple of years later the Coffee House was destroyed by fire. But its ruins were regarded by the local people as being still haunted for a long time after the disaster.

Perhaps the most famous of all haunted houses in Scotland is the House of Inverawe, near Loch Etive in Argyll. Certainly its strange story appears in many books written about ghosts in Britain. This building has an association with Fort Ticonderoga, which lies at the junction of Lakes George and Champlain, between the States of New York and Vermont. In the year 1758 a fierce attack was made on the fort in which Highland troops (the 42nd Highlanders) were engaged and received severe losses in both dead and wounded. One of those who received fatal injuries was Major Duncan Campbell of Inverawe. The transatlantic association arises from the story that one night the ghost of a murdered brother appeared to Duncan Campbell. It informed him that one of the latter's guests in the house was Stuart of Appin, the brother's murderer. The ghost tried to persuade Duncan to take some kind of revenue while Stuart was still in the building. But the old Highland code of hospitality, recognised for centuries and which applied to all under a man's roof no matter what they had done, was too strong to be violated. Campbell could not go against the code, even under such circumstances. In vain the ghost appealed. But Duncan remained resolute. Disappointed, the ghost left, but before it disappeared it uttered a word which had never before been heard in Iverawe, nor even in all of Argyll: 'Ticonderoga.'

Some time after this incident, Duncan Campbell of Inverawe joined the 42nd Highlanders and he eventually found himself in America with many of his kinsmen. And, as the ghost of his dead brother had predicted, Campbell was killed there at the fort on 17 July, 1758.

The story does not end there. On the very day that Campbell fell mortally wounded, two of his male relatives, father and son, were asleep in far-off Inverawe House, each in separate beds. That night the son awoke to find a figure crossing the bedroom floor. The tall, ghostly figure, dressed in Highland military uniform, stooped over his father's bed. Terrified at the sight, the boy hid himself under the bedclothes and remained like this until daylight. In the morning he told his father what he had seen and was told in return that it had been the ghost of their kinsman, Duncan Campbell, who had come to give the news of his own death and that of a number of men who had been killed with him in the action at Ticonderoga (the actual number was mentioned: 8 officers, 9 sergeants, and 297 men).

It was several weeks before the news of the battle eventually reached this country, confirming both the name of Ticonderoga and the number slain. Since then the ghost is said to have haunted the house on many occasions.

Half-way up Scotland's longest glen, Glen Lyon, stands Meggernie Castle. The oldest parts of the building date from the fifteenth century and, in keeping with one's expectations of ancient castles, the ghost of the castle is no little-known spirit. Its first recorded manifestations date from 1862 when two men staying at the castle each had an experience which they related the following morning independently in order to obtain some comparison.

In essence, each man had been awakened by what had felt like a hot kiss upon his cheek, so hot and searing that it seemed as if the burn had gone right through to the cheekbone. On leaping out of bed, the upper half of a ghostly woman's body was seen by each of the men going straight through a locked and sealed-off door which, when tried, remained as fast as it had always been. Looking in the mirror, there was no sign of any burn, nor of any sign which could account for the tingling sensation still in the cheek.

The curiosity of the incident was heightened by reports from some of the castle servants who claimed to have seen the *lower* part of a woman's body flitting about the corridors. This part in fact had been seen also by many people locally, particularly when in the vicinity of a nearby graveyard. The ghost was seen on occasions afterwards, but only its upper half.

These independent sightings tended to confirm an incident which, by the 19th century, had passed into the corpus of local folklore in Glen Lyon, when one of the chiefs of the Clan Menzies murdered his young and beautiful wife. In an effort to hide the evidence of his crime, he cut the body in two parts and concealed them in an old cabinet which stood in a closet room located between the rooms which the two men already mentioned were to occupy years later in 1862. Under the cover of darkness, the murderer managed to remove the lower half of his wife's body to the graveyard nearby and bury it there. But on the night he endeavoured to remove to the same place the upper half of his victim's body, he himself was found murdered, doubtless by someone who was aware of the crime he had committed. No one was ever charged with the chief's death and, indeed, the assassin's identification was never sought officially.

Late last century, when some repairs were being carried out in the castle, a skeleton head and shoulders were found which were removed to outside the castle and given a Christian burial.

Many years ago a house in Forrest Road, Edinburgh, had the reputation of being haunted, but the stories were frequently put down to idle gossip. In the basement were the usual kitchen offices and cellars; otherwise the house was no different in appearance from its neighbours. After a new owner had been in the house for some weeks, she became gradually aware of a strange, sweet odour in one of the cellars. After confirming that the smell had no physical origin, she decided that the matter merited closer investigation. One evening she took herself and her two dogs down to the cellars. But at the entrance the dogs suddenly cowered to the floor and refused to accompany her any further. Taking this as an indication that perhaps there was something unusual about the house she had bought, and thinking that there was some substance to the local stories about the place, she carried out a very close inspection of ceiling, walls and floor.

It was not until she had thoroughly examined the floor of the cellar that she noticed that part was unmistakably of more recent origin than the rest. As she looked closer she became aware of the atmosphere becoming increasingly damp and in some way heavy and intense, which struck her as odd because the floors and walls were singularly dry. Almost at once, as she rapped the walls of the cellar with a gritty determination, a great wave of a sickly-sweet smell overpowered her. The flame of the candle she was holding, the only light she had in the cellar, turned a cold blue. A crashing noise made her turn round, but there was nothing she could see which could account for such a noise. She tried to call out to her dogs, but found her throat muscles paralysed.

As she stood rooted to the spot, unable to do anything but to wait for the unknown, her eyes caught the sight of a faint glow at the top of the cellar stairs. It had the same light as a phosphorescent glimmer and the shape gradually became more defined; it was short and squat and appeared to be partly clad in a loose, flowing garment which was not long enough to wholly conceal the legs. The shape glided over the cellar floor noiselessly and then halted, it seemed to the owner of the house, over that part of the floor where the newer tiles were laid. As it stood there for a moment, there was a loud crashing sound as though the whole house were falling down into a heap of rubble. Then the onlooker fainted. When she recovered, the cellar was empty of both ghost and sound.

A week passed and nothing further was either seen or heard. Then one night, when the owner of the house had fallen asleep, she was suddenly awakened with a start. The same sweet odour as she had experienced in the cellar was now just as strong in her bedroom. As she forced herself to open her eyes with the intention to investigate its source, she was confronted by a ghostly face staring down at her. The sight was so horrific that she almost succumbed to her fear. Then, as the sweet and sickly odour increased in intensity, the image receded and grew fainter until it disappeared altogether.

After that experience, it was decided to investigate the past history of her property. Her efforts were rewarded by the discovery of records which revealed that the site of her house had been originally occupied by a small cottage in which lived two sisters, both nurses, one of whom had been suspected of poisoning the other. The cottage, due to the parsimonious habits of the owners, eventually got into such a bad state of repair that it was blown down during a violent storm, the surviving sister perishing in the ruins.

Glamis Castle, the ancestral home of the Earl of Strathmore and the birthplace of Princess Margaret, is a typically haunted Scottish castle which has many ghosts. These spirits have been seen over many centuries by a number of different people whose accounts, while differing in detail, coincide in their fundamental points. There is the ghost of the tormented Jane Douglas, who was burnt at the stake in the sixteenth century for allegedly conspiring with others to murder King James V. The other spirit is that of the profligate Earl Baerdie, who is said to have staked his soul in a game of chance with the Devil and who enacts his penance by playing an endless game in a secret room which is said to exist, though it has never been discovered.

The ghost of Lady Hamilton of Bothwellhaugh is said to haunt the surrounding countryside. In her time, while her husband was away from home, a favourite of the Regent Moray seized the house and plundered the building. Lady Hamilton was turned outside, naked and terrified, into the open fields where, when the following morning dawned, she was found raving mad, with her dead infant beside her.

A house in Edinburgh, near St Mary's Place, is said to be haunted by a ghostly dog. The wife of a past occupant was reading quietly one day when she was astonished to see, floating in the air, the apparition of the head of an old man. Later both she and her husband had the experience of seeing the head, together with the head of a child, and a pale, disembodied arm reaching out as though to grasp the two heads. On another occasion, the family were disturbed to see a ghostly black dog which would jump onto a chair before vanishing from their sight.

Many years ago the photograph of what came to be known as the 'Spectral Face of Liberton' caused some comment. Liberton House, in the Midlothian parish of the same name, has a large hall with several interesting features. There is an ancient nail-studded door framed in stone and a similarly-framed recess above it. One of the many tenants of the building decided to engage a professional photographer to take pictures of the building and the hall in particular. This was carried out, and when one photograph of the hall had been developed there appeared in one corner, near the above-mentioned recess, the shape of a huge human face. It had a well-shaped nose, down-turned eyes under heavy eyebrows, and a mouth which had a slow, enigmatic smile. The mystery was that while the face was obvious on the photograph, it was not so apparent on the wall itself. The locus of the apparition was investigated carefully but nothing was found save a stretch of dirty and discoloured plaster.

The photograph was duly sent to a principal photographic journal for investigation and comment. The verdict was cautious: 'We cannot be expected, on the evidence before us, to admit that it is really a " ghost." But we do not think it in the least probable that the glass had been used before (it was a plate glass camera which had been used); for no professional photographer would use a glass twice. We believe it would be possible (we cannot say more) to produce a very similar effect by a minute pin-hole in the camera or bellows. We are glad to have had the opportunity of seeing what is, beyond doubt, a distinct curiosity.' The general opinion, however, discounted the pin-hole theory, and the mystery still remains to this day.

Another ghost-haunted house takes us back to the reign of Charles II. It concerns Spedlins Tower, near Applegarth. In one of the dungeons of the tower, a miller named Porteous was imprisoned, being suspected of arson. The owner of the Tower, Sir Alexander Jardine, saw to it that his prisoner was safely locked up before arranging for a trial. But the following day Jardine was called unexpectedly to Edinburgh and rode post haste for the capital — with the dungeon keys in his pocket. In due course he remembered his unfortunate prisoner. But by that time the miller had died of starvation.

Almost immediately after this occurred, the miller's ghost began to trouble the household, screaming and crying out in need of food to eat. Eventually a priest was sent for to perform an exorcism which was successful in driving the ghost out of the family's quarters and back to the dungeons. One of the articles used in the ceremony was a large black-lettered Bible and it was under-

stood by the family that so long as this Bible
remained in the house the ghost would not be able
to haunt them again. For many years the Bible was
kept safely in Spedlins Tower until there arose the
occasion for it to be sent to Edinburgh for re-
binding. Although by this time the family of Jardine
had moved to a new house nearby, the ghost made
straight for the new building and remained there,
in a reign of terror, until the Bible was replaced in
Spedlins Tower again. The ghost was well known
in the area and became a source of entertainment
to those who had courage enough to descend to the
dungeons to hear what was described as terrible
screams and the fluttering of a bird. Later the story
was told of person who pushed a thin twig through
the keyhole of the cell, then to draw it back to find
the bark stripped as though by the teeth of a
ravenous ghost. This tale more than likely records
the essence of the treatment which the unfortunate
miller got from his cruel and inhuman guards.

An old building on the outskirts of Inverness has
been recently converted into a hotel. In the last
year or two it has given certain sensitive persons
experiences which indicate that it is haunted. One
American saw one evening the ghostly shape of a
monk, but thought no more of the matter until he
heard later that the same figure was seen by another
independent person and at a different time; he has
since made arrangements to revisit the hotel.

Despite the ever-increasing tendency towards
materialism in our society today, the ghost still
makes its appearance and hardly a month goes by

without some mention in the press of a haunting, a sighting or a series of unexplained and mysterious noises.

The cottage known as Ben Alder Cottage, down the side of Loch Ericht, south-west of Dalwhinnie, Inverness-shire, is reckoned to be one of the loneliest houses in Scotland. For many years the building had stood as a derelict habitation, though it served as a rough shelter for climbers and wandering folk who sought refuge from all kinds of bad weather.

Recently two climbers decided to use the cottage for an overnight stay. About nine o'clock in the evening they were bedding themselves down by candlelight when they heard tappings on the outside door. They were no ordinary tappings, however; rather they were loud, rapid, staccato raps as though from long and hard fingernails. The sounds were followed by others from the room at the other end of the cottage; heavy, slow footfalls on bare wood boards. But the climbers knew the room was quite empty. The footfalls were subsequently replaced by the sounds of furniture being moved across the floor. The whole house reverberated with the noise. For fifteen minutes the two climbers sat in the middle of these aural manifestations which ended with a series of protracted and agonised human groans. They would have gladly left the cottage for other shelter were it not for the fact that there was none such for miles around.

By the time the morning light had arrived, Rannoch Moor was being lashed with wind and rain. The climbers investigated the outside of the house, but found no trace of anything which could have explained the noises of the previous night.

As they made preparations to continue their journey, one of the climbers decided to leave behind ' payment ' in the form of a packet of biscuits for anyone else who might arrive at the cottage for shelter and be short of something to eat. It was a large, cylindrical packet and it was no sooner placed on the mantelshelf when it flew right across the room to land on the floor — upright, and as steady as though placed there by a careful human hand.

On another occasion, some climbers had the experience of seeing the front door burst open (it was a heavy double door which could be locked with bolts top and bottom), though there was no wind outside. And subsequent noises sounded to the visitors as though very large packages were being dropped on the floor. A nomad who frequents these hills in the Ben Alder region recounts the story of one night spent in the cottage being interrupted by a voice outside which kept crying for help. Though it was bright moonlight, the tramp searched in vain for a trace of someone.

A council house in Irvine, Ayrshire, has not escaped the attention of ghostly visits. This particular ghost has defied the attempts of a priest to exorcise it. A few days after the family had moved into the house, in 1968, the housewife saw an elderly woman dressed in white who asked her what the family was doing in her (the ghost's) house, and warned her that if they stayed they would have bad luck. The ghost was described as being a woman, in her seventies, dressed in a long white gown with frilled lace cuffs. She continually toyed with a heavy gold wedding ring and her appearances are always heralded by the smell of cheap perfume throughout the house. This ghost has been seen by other members of the same family.

Another ghost of the seventies haunts the second floor of a hotel in Dumfries. Footsteps are heard when no one is in the corridor. At other times, a shimmering white figure is seen flitting about and passing through a wall where there was once a door. The ghost is described as being dressed in white with a serene, rather sad look on her face. Those who see her also hear the rustle of her petticoats as she walks the corridor. A medium was called in to investigate the haunting. She discovered that the ghost was in fact a friendly spirit and meant no harm to any living person. With this professional assurance, the family in the hotel have decided to live with their spirit rather than have her removed by holding a seance.

POSTSCRIPT

THE general survey of paranormal manifestations
provided in this book will no doubt stir in the minds
of most readers memories of similar or other types
of happenings either within the context of their own
experience, or of stories conveyed to them by friends
and acquaintances. It is generally believed that the
incidence of the 'unexplained' is much higher than
one might be led to expect in a society such as ours
which is so technology-orientated, and one in which
belief in one or other of the established religions
tends increasingly to be more the exception rather
than the rule. That this is so must firstly indicate
that there are severe and practical limits to the
known areas in which the average human being
operates; but that outside these limits, which in
many cases are merely perimeters of belief, there
exists a dimension involving time — perhaps an
elevated mental plane on which only those with
special assimilative and participatory gifts can
operate. However, it is commonly thought that
these gifts can be developed by study and practice,
not perhaps through the use of 'black arts,' but
through a determined effort on the part of an
individual to create the necessary environmental
conditions in which a further sense, sixth or even

seventh, can make contact with the residual evidence of a former existence.

There are a number of experience types, such as déja vu, for instance, which are certainly not confined to the more sensitive individual who has had his or her gifts confirmed by the evidence of definite contacts. Regularly, in the popular press, one reads accounts of the experience of ordinary people who, in a certain environment, created by a number of contributory and inter-related factors, have made contact with ' something ' which was quite unexpected and outside the normal well-established patterns of life and living. Thus it is the author's belief that the more people who come forward to relate first-hand experiences the sooner we, in our own fixed and rigid time-scale, will come to a better understanding of those things which are at one and the same time in both our past and in our future. While this book hopes to entertain, it also hopes to stimulate further thinking about a subject which has occupied the mind of finite man for thousands of years. If it has done both, it will have served a useful purpose.